MATHS PLUS
FROM HEINEMANN

Teaching Mental Maths Strategies 5

Len Frobisher

John Threlfall

Heinemann

Heinemann Educational Publishers
Halley Court, Jordan Hill, Oxford OX2 8EJ
a division of Reed Educational and Professional Publishing Ltd

Heinemann is a registered trademark of Reed Educational and Professional Publishing Ltd

OXFORD ATHENS FLORENCE PRAGUE MADRID
MELBOURNE AUCKLAND SINGAPORE TOKYO SAO PAULO
CHICAGO PORTSMOUTH (NH) MEXICO IBADAN KUALA LUMPUR
GABORONE JOHANNESBURG KAMPALA NAIROBI

First published 1998

01 00 99 98
10 9 8 7 6 5 4 3 2 1

ISBN 0 435 02426 4

Designed and typeset by AMR Ltd
Illustrated by AMR Ltd
Cover design by Phil Leafe
Printed and bound by Thomson Litho Ltd, Scotland

Contents

Introduction

The *Teaching Mental Maths Strategies* series has been written to help teachers develop their pupils' mental arithmetic skills. Skill in mental arithmetic

- is an important part of any mathematics curriculum
- is a useful tool in everyday life
- provides a base for developing other aspects of mathematics
- gives children confidence in the early learning of mathematics
- supports problem-solving skills.

Building up mental strategies

Children can construct their own mental strategies to perform calculations without being taught to do so. This series offers an organised sequence of teaching activities to help make children's strategies more efficient and powerful. It provides a structured progression from simple numbers to larger and more complex numbers.

Developing children's strategies

The approach used in *Teaching Mental Maths Strategies* is based on an understanding that children can more easily develop their own ways of working things out if there is careful support from the teacher. For example, this might include:

- encouraging and valuing children's suggestions
- organising the children so that they listen to each other
- encouraging children to be aware of a wide range of mental strategies
- discussing the mathematical reasons why a strategy works
- maintaining a high level of expectation.

The aim is for you and the children to be continually suggesting new possibilities, rather than following prescribed methods. Different children will develop different strategies for the same problem, and the same child may have different strategies for apparently similar problems. The important thing is that all children have a repertoire of strategies that they can apply to a variety of problems, and be able to describe their strategies and also explain why they work.

The structure of the book

Teaching Mental Maths Strategies is structured as a series of two-page units of work which each represent roughly a week's teaching. A half-term of work is therefore provided in the material numbered 3.1 to 3.6 (or 2.1 to 2.6, and so on).

There are three different types of unit in the book:

- **Building strategies**
- **Using strategies**
- **Looking back, Looking forward**.

The sequence of units in a half-term could therefore be

Looking forward (one week)

Building strategies (two weeks)

Using strategies (one week)

Building strategies (two weeks)

Using strategies (one week)

Looking back (one week)

Symbols used in the book

The following symbols guide you through the lessons:

 starter question to read to the class

 symbolise a child's strategy

 practice questions

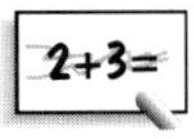

record on the board

Building strategies

These units are the core of the book, introducing and developing the strategies. The left-hand page is information to familiarise you with the content of the unit and the possible strategies for this kind of problem. The right-hand page describes what you can do in three 10-minute sessions, if possible on three successive days. A typical Building strategies unit:

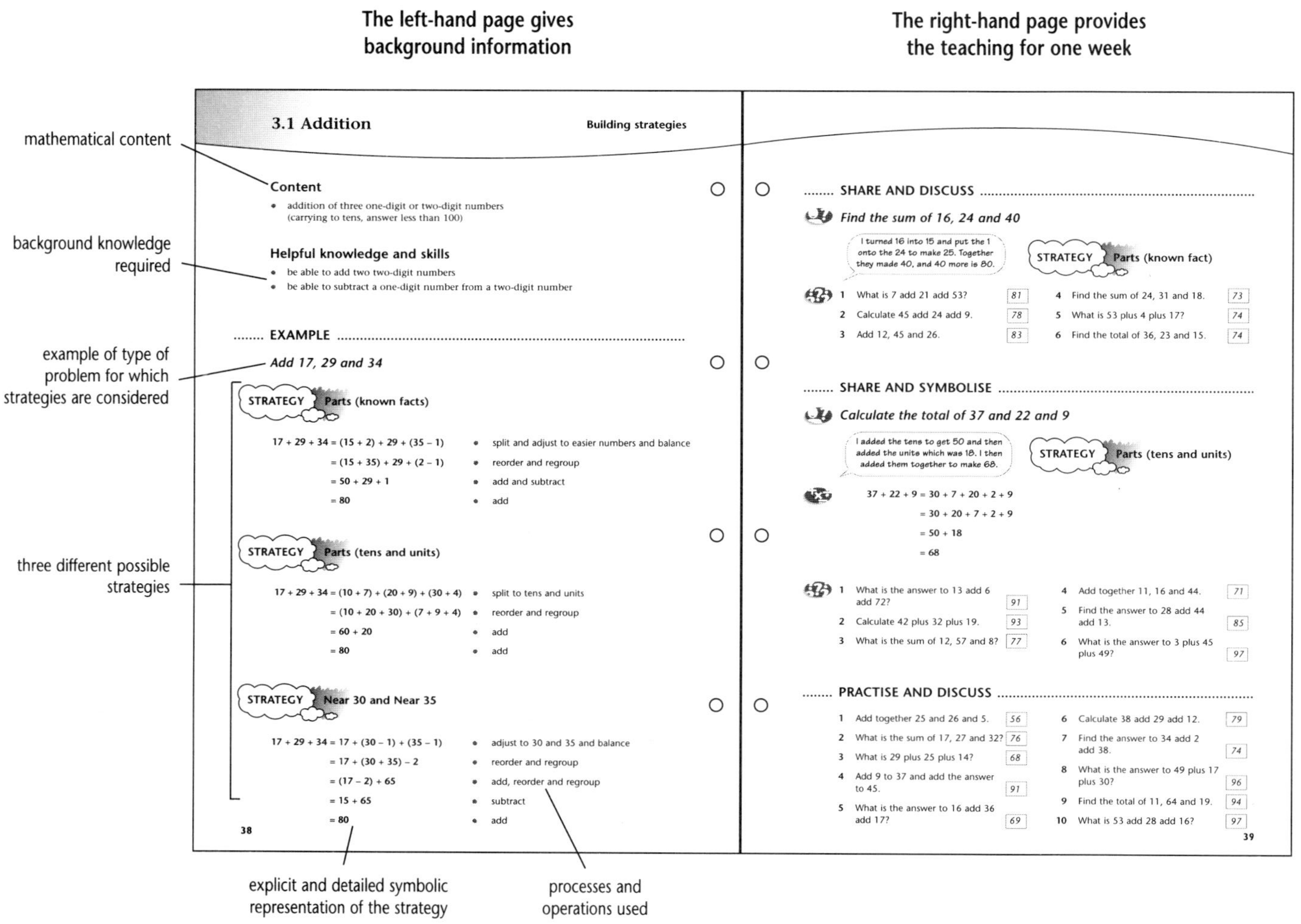

3.1 Addition — Building strategies

Content
- addition of three one-digit or two-digit numbers (carrying to tens, answer less than 100)

Helpful knowledge and skills
- be able to add two two-digit numbers
- be able to subtract a one-digit number from a two-digit number

.... EXAMPLE ....

Add 17, 29 and 34

STRATEGY Parts (known facts)

17 + 29 + 34 = (15 + 2) + 29 + (35 − 1)	• split and adjust to easier numbers and balance
= (15 + 35) + 29 + (2 − 1)	• reorder and regroup
= 50 + 29 + 1	• add and subtract
= 80	• add

STRATEGY Parts (tens and units)

17 + 29 + 34 = (10 + 7) + (20 + 9) + (30 + 4)	• split to tens and units
= (10 + 20 + 30) + (7 + 9 + 4)	• reorder and regroup
= 60 + 20	• add
= 80	• add

STRATEGY Near 30 and Near 35

17 + 29 + 34 = 17 + (30 − 1) + (35 − 1)	• adjust to 30 and 35 and balance
= 17 + (30 + 35) − 2	• reorder and regroup
= (17 − 2) + 65	• add, reorder and regroup
= 15 + 65	• subtract
= 80	• add

38

.... SHARE AND DISCUSS ....

Find the sum of 16, 24 and 40

I turned 16 into 15 and put the 1 onto the 24 to make 25. Together they made 40, and 40 more is 80.

STRATEGY Parts (known fact)

1 What is 7 add 21 add 53? 81
2 Calculate 45 add 24 add 9. 78
3 Add 12, 45 and 26. 83
4 Find the sum of 24, 31 and 18. 73
5 What is 53 plus 4 plus 17? 74
6 Find the total of 36, 23 and 15. 74

.... SHARE AND SYMBOLISE ....

Calculate the total of 37 and 22 and 9

I added the tens to get 50 and then added the units which was 18. I then added them together to make 68.

STRATEGY Parts (tens and units)

37 + 22 + 9 = 30 + 7 + 20 + 2 + 9
= 30 + 20 + 7 + 2 + 9
= 50 + 18
= 68

1 What is the answer to 13 add 6 add 72? 91
2 Calculate 42 plus 32 plus 19. 93
3 What is the sum of 12, 57 and 8? 77
4 Add together 11, 16 and 44. 71
5 Find the answer to 28 add 44 add 13. 85
6 What is the answer to 3 plus 45 plus 49? 97

.... PRACTISE AND DISCUSS ....

1 Add together 25 and 26 and 5. 56
2 What is the sum of 17, 27 and 32? 76
3 What is 29 plus 25 plus 14? 68
4 Add 9 to 37 and add the answer to 45. 91
5 What is the answer to 16 add 36 add 17? 69
6 Calculate 38 add 29 add 12. 79
7 Find the answer to 34 add 2 add 38. 74
8 What is the answer to 49 plus 17 plus 30? 96
9 Find the total of 11, 64 and 19. 94
10 What is 53 add 28 add 16? 97

39

first session: Share and discuss

- starter problem – read out and ask the children to solve this mentally, allowing the children to share and discuss their strategies
- record one child's strategy for all to talk about (one child's response is provided as an illustration, which may be used by the teacher, if appropriate)
- practice problems – read out for the children to solve, putting the numbers on the board as reminders. Some of the strategies used for one problem could be discussed at this point.

second session: Share and symbolise

- discuss and record one example, allowing children to share and discuss their strategies
- record one child's strategy for all to talk about
- write up the child's strategy in symbols on the board, and question the children to make sure they understand the mathematics of the strategy
- practice problems – some of the strategies used for one problem could be discussed at this point.

third session: Practise and discuss

- read out the problems, and discuss some of the strategies used – an opportunity to evaluate children's developing strategies.
- answers are given on the page

Using strategies

These units set mental strategies in a wider mathematical context, and use more complex problems.

The left-hand page

Investigations provide open-ended problems related to the content of the previous Building strategies units. These Investigations develop an appreciation of the number patterns and relationships that underpin mental strategies through two or three 10-minute sessions.

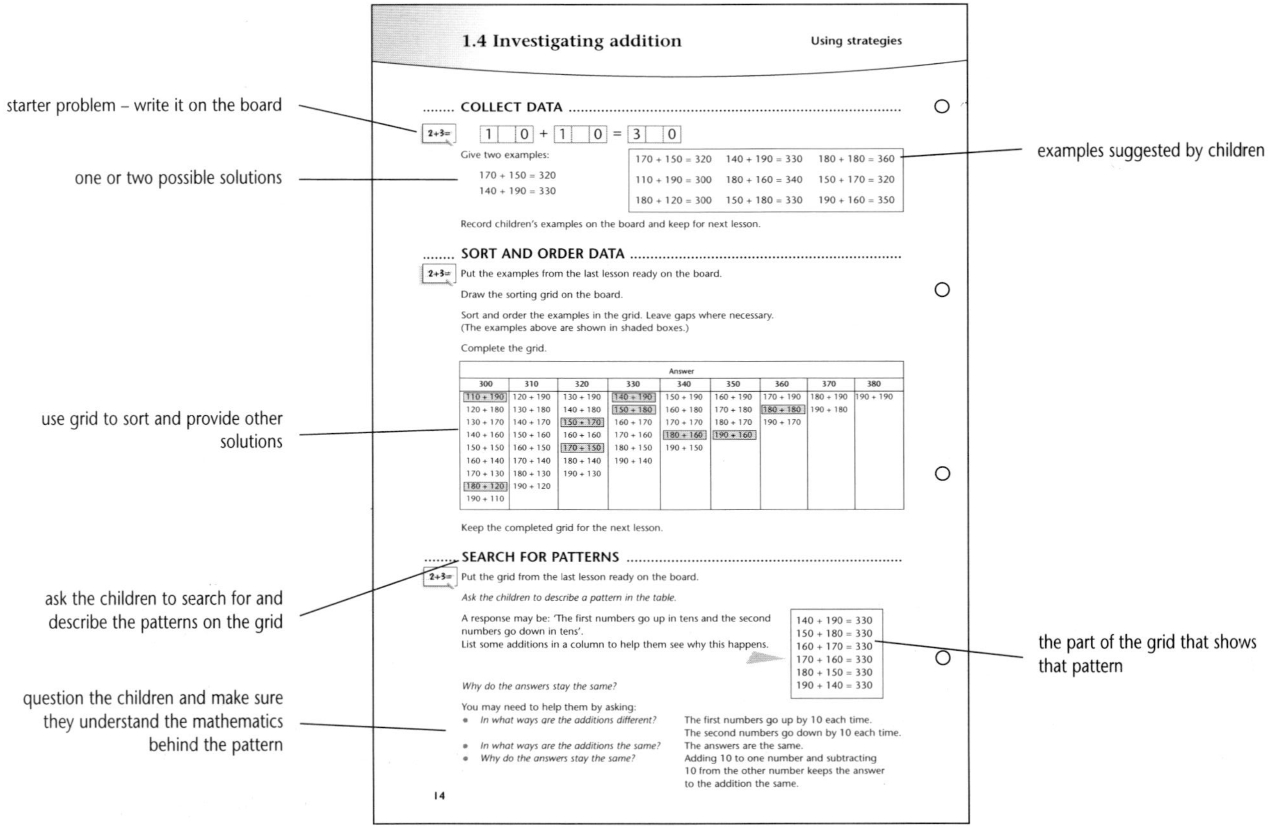

1.4 Investigating addition — Using strategies

COLLECT DATA

2+3= 1 0 + 1 0 = 3 0

Give two examples:

170 + 150 = 320
140 + 190 = 330

170 + 150 = 320	140 + 190 = 330	180 + 180 = 360
110 + 190 = 300	180 + 160 = 340	150 + 170 = 320
180 + 120 = 300	150 + 180 = 330	190 + 160 = 350

Record children's examples on the board and keep for next lesson.

SORT AND ORDER DATA

2+3= Put the examples from the last lesson ready on the board.

Draw the sorting grid on the board.

Sort and order the examples in the grid. Leave gaps where necessary. (The examples above are shown in shaded boxes.)

Complete the grid.

Answer								
300	310	320	330	340	350	360	370	380
110 + 190	120 + 190	130 + 190	140 + 190	150 + 190	160 + 190	170 + 190	180 + 190	190 + 190
120 + 180	130 + 180	140 + 180	150 + 180	160 + 180	170 + 180	180 + 180	190 + 180	
130 + 170	140 + 170	150 + 170	160 + 170	170 + 170	180 + 170	190 + 170		
140 + 160	150 + 160	160 + 160	170 + 160	180 + 160	190 + 160			
150 + 150	160 + 150	170 + 150	180 + 150	190 + 150				
160 + 140	170 + 140	180 + 140	190 + 140					
170 + 130	180 + 130	190 + 130						
180 + 120	190 + 120							
190 + 110								

Keep the completed grid for the next lesson.

SEARCH FOR PATTERNS

2+3= Put the grid from the last lesson ready on the board.

Ask the children to describe a pattern in the table.

A response may be: 'The first numbers go up in tens and the second numbers go down in tens'.
List some additions in a column to help them see why this happens.

140 + 190 = 330
150 + 180 = 330
160 + 170 = 330
170 + 160 = 330
180 + 150 = 330
190 + 140 = 330

Why do the answers stay the same?

You may need to help them by asking:
- *In what ways are the additions different?*
- *In what ways are the additions the same?*
- *Why do the answers stay the same?*

The first numbers go up by 10 each time.
The second numbers go down by 10 each time.
The answers are the same.
Adding 10 to one number and subtracting 10 from the other number keeps the answer to the addition the same.

14

The right-hand page

Mathematics problems and **Word problems** help children apply their strategies. Mathematics problems are designed to be used in two 10-minute verbal/oral sessions, and may require the children to think about what calculations to perform as well as what strategy to use.

Word problems are presented orally, and the children have to decide which operation to use. The page guides you in how to present the strategy visually, as many children will find this helpful. Word problems pages are intended to take one 10-minute session, but can be split into two sessions if necessary.

1.4 Mathematics problem: Half-way between — Using strategies

mathematical content

Content
- how to approach 'half-way' questions

starter problem – read and ask the children how they worked it out

EXAMPLE

What number is half-way between 350 and 580? 465

Picture this:

draw one child's method to discuss and stimulate other mental representations

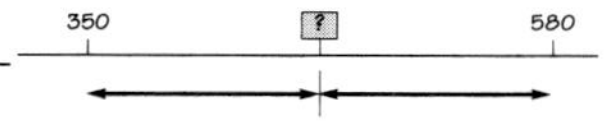

Add half the difference to the smaller number.

practice questions – children try out their own mental pictures

1. What is half-way between 185 and 395? 290
2. What is half-way between 850 and 420? 635
3. What is half-way between 406 and 512? 459
4. What is half-way between 532 and 764? 648
5. What is half-way between 140 and 980? 560
6. What is half-way between 358 and 564? 461

starter problem related to the previous one

EXAMPLE

What number is half-way between 102 and 408? 255

Picture this:

draw and discuss one child's methods

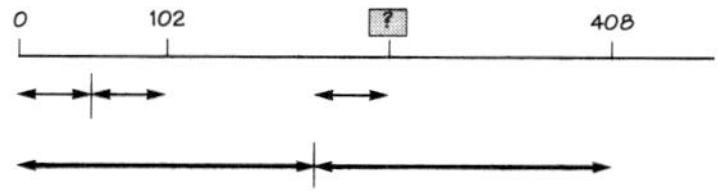

Add together half of each (or halve the sum of both).

1. What is half-way between 68 and 140? 104
2. What is half-way between 206 and 404? 305
3. What is half-way between 66 and 520? 293
4. What is half-way between 160 and 320? 240
5. What is half-way between 250 and 660? 455
6. What is half-way between 242 and 826? 534

15

1.7 Word problems — Using strategies

starter problem – children discuss how they knew what operation to perform

Simon's book has a mass of 730 grams. Sara's book has a mass of 580 grams. How many more grams is Simon's book than Sara's? 150 g

Picture a balance:

show the children a visual representation of the relationships between the numbers in the problem

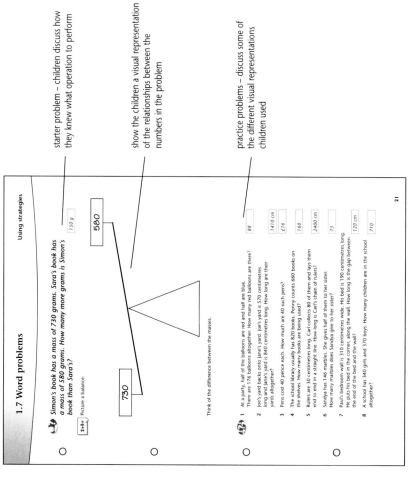

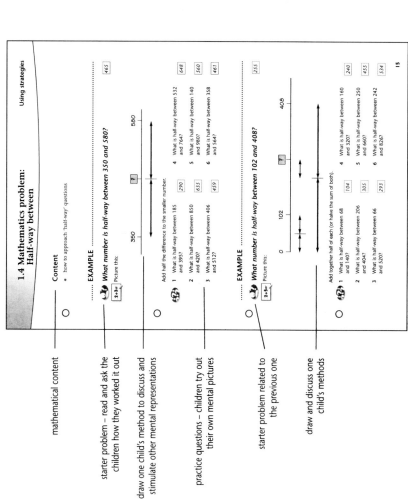

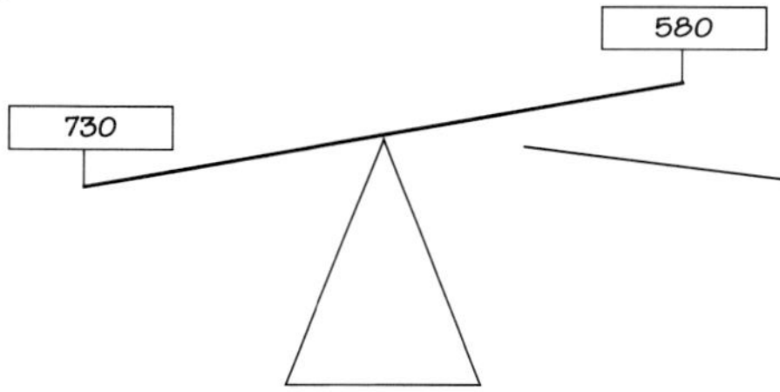

Think of the difference between the masses.

practice problems – discuss some of the different visual representations children used

1. At a party, half of the balloons are red and half are blue. There are 176 balloons altogether. How many red balloons are there? 88
2. Joe's yard backs onto Jane's yard. Joe's yard is 570 centimetres long and Jane's yard is 840 centimetres long. How long are their yards altogether? 1410 cm
3. Pens cost 40 pence each. How much are 40 such pens? £16
4. The school library usually has 820 books. Penny counts 660 books on the shelves. How many books are being used? 160
5. Rulers are 30 centimetres long. Carl collects 80 of them and lays them end to end in a straight line. How long is Carl's chain of rulers? 2400 cm
6. Sandya has 146 marbles. She gives half of them to her sister. How many marbles does Sandya give to her sister? 73
7. Paul's bedroom wall is 310 centimetres wide. His bed is 190 centimetres long. He puts his bed in the corner, along the wall. How long is the gap between the end of the bed and the wall? 120 cm
8. A school has 340 girls and 370 boys. How many children are in the school altogether? 710

21

Looking back, Looking forward

These units round off a half-term of work and prepare for the next one. **Looking back** pages assess progress so far, and **Looking forward** pages find out whether the children have the necessary background knowledge for the next half-term of work. The answers to Looking back are given on page 94.

Looking back

Each Looking back page has two sets of questions to assess whether the children have developed efficient, effective and accurate mental strategies in the previous half-term's work.

You can photocopy the pages and give out the sheets so the children can read the questions and write the answers in the boxes, or you may read the questions to the children who write the answers either in the boxes or in an exercise book. You may choose whether or not to allow the children to do a limited amount of working out on paper.

The completed Looking back pages can be used diagnostically and/or kept as a summary of progress.

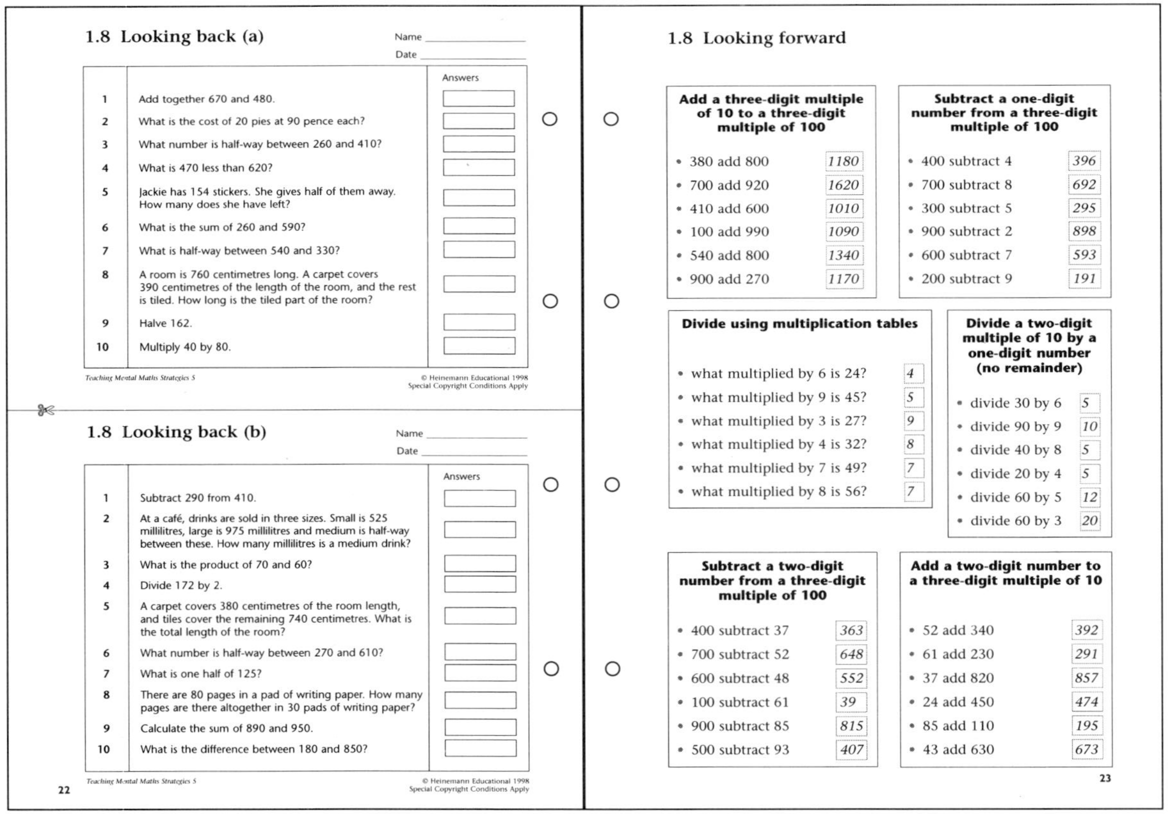

1.8 Looking back (a)

Name ______
Date ______

		Answers
1	Add together 670 and 480.	
2	What is the cost of 20 pies at 90 pence each?	
3	What number is half-way between 260 and 410?	
4	What is 470 less than 620?	
5	Jackie has 154 stickers. She gives half of them away. How many does she have left?	
6	What is the sum of 260 and 590?	
7	What is half-way between 540 and 330?	
8	A room is 760 centimetres long. A carpet covers 390 centimetres of the length of the room, and the rest is tiled. How long is the tiled part of the room?	
9	Halve 162.	
10	Multiply 40 by 80.	

Teaching Mental Maths Strategies 5

© Heinemann Educational 1998 Special Copyright Conditions Apply

1.8 Looking back (b)

Name ______
Date ______

		Answers
1	Subtract 290 from 410.	
2	At a café, drinks are sold in three sizes. Small is 525 millilitres, large is 975 millilitres and medium is half-way between these. How many millilitres is a medium drink?	
3	What is the product of 70 and 60?	
4	Divide 172 by 2.	
5	A carpet covers 380 centimetres of the room length, and tiles cover the remaining 740 centimetres. What is the total length of the room?	
6	What number is half-way between 270 and 610?	
7	What is one half of 125?	
8	There are 80 pages in a pad of writing paper. How many pages are there altogether in 30 pads of writing paper?	
9	Calculate the sum of 890 and 950.	
10	What is the difference between 180 and 850?	

22 Teaching Mental Maths Strategies 5

© Heinemann Educational 1998 Special Copyright Conditions Apply

1.8 Looking forward

Add a three-digit multiple of 10 to a three-digit multiple of 100

- 380 add 800 *1180*
- 700 add 920 *1620*
- 410 add 600 *1010*
- 100 add 990 *1090*
- 540 add 800 *1340*
- 900 add 270 *1170*

Subtract a one-digit number from a three-digit multiple of 100

- 400 subtract 4 *396*
- 700 subtract 8 *692*
- 300 subtract 5 *295*
- 900 subtract 2 *898*
- 600 subtract 7 *593*
- 200 subtract 9 *191*

Divide using multiplication tables

- what multiplied by 6 is 24? *4*
- what multiplied by 9 is 45? *5*
- what multiplied by 3 is 27? *9*
- what multiplied by 4 is 32? *8*
- what multiplied by 7 is 49? *7*
- what multiplied by 8 is 56? *7*

Divide a two-digit multiple of 10 by a one-digit number (no remainder)

- divide 30 by 6 *5*
- divide 90 by 9 *10*
- divide 40 by 8 *5*
- divide 20 by 4 *5*
- divide 60 by 5 *12*
- divide 60 by 3 *20*

Subtract a two-digit number from a three-digit multiple of 100

- 400 subtract 37 *363*
- 700 subtract 52 *648*
- 600 subtract 48 *552*
- 100 subtract 61 *39*
- 900 subtract 85 *815*
- 500 subtract 93 *407*

Add a two-digit number to a three-digit multiple of 10

- 52 add 340 *392*
- 61 add 230 *291*
- 37 add 820 *857*
- 24 add 450 *474*
- 85 add 110 *195*
- 43 add 630 *673*

23

Looking forward

These pages have six sets of short questions to test the mathematical knowledge needed in the forthcoming half-term. You read out the questions and the children calculate mentally and respond orally or in writing as appropriate.

The strategies: **parts** and **near**

The mental strategies developed in *Teaching Mental Maths Strategies* are based upon two main processes:

- **parts** – splitting or adjusting a number in various ways to make a calculation easier to perform
- **near** – changing a number to another number near to it.

Parts strategies

Parts strategies are usually followed in brackets by a description of the operation that produced the parts. The following example shows the strategy **parts (isolate 350)** in which both the 650 and the 380 are split into 350 and another number, so that the 350s match

650 – 380 = 300 + 350 – 350 – 30	• split to isolate 350s
= 300 – 30	• subtract
= 270	• subtract

The child who devised this strategy saw that it was easier to subtract if the numbers were split into more manageable parts.

Another strategy, **parts (tens and units)**, devised by a different child for the same problem involved splitting the two numbers into tens and units

650 – 380 = 600 + 50 – 300 – 80	• split to tens and units
= (600 – 300) + (50 – 80)	• reorder and regroup
= 300 – 30	• subtract
= 270	• subtract

Near strategies

Near strategies are usually followed by a number, such as **near 100**, or **near 1600** in this example

$\frac{1}{2}$ of 1500 = $\frac{1}{2}$ of (1600 – 100)	• adjust to 1600 and balance
= $\frac{1}{2}$ of 1600 – $\frac{1}{2}$ of 100	• regroup (distributive law)
= 800 – 50	• halves
= 750	• subtract

The strategies that are used in *Teaching Mental Maths Strategies* 5 are listed below.

parts
parts (known facts)
parts (tens and units)
parts (hundreds and tens)
parts (hundreds, tens and units)
parts (hundreds, and tens and units)
parts (thousands and hundreds)
parts (thousands, hundreds and tens)
parts (match tens)
parts (match hundreds)
parts (complement)
parts (isolate a 10)
parts (isolate a 100)
parts (isolate 270)
parts (isolate 350)
parts (isolate 600)
parts (factors)
parts (factor of 2)
parts (factor of 10)
parts (factor of 100)
near 10
near 30
near 35
near 60
near 63
near 70
near 80
near 90
near 100
near 140
near 200
near 300
near 400
near 500
near 600
near 800
near 900
near 1000
near 1600
double

The strategy 'double' is a highly specific strategy that applies to a very limited type of problem.

1.1 Looking back (a)

Name ____________________

Date ____________________

		Answers
1	Calculate 643 subtract 9.	
2	What is 73 multiplied by 2?	
3	Two classes collected used stamps for charity. One class collected 500 stamps. The other class collected 940 stamps. How many stamps were collected altogether?	
4	Find one half of 65.	
5	What is 6 add 478?	
6	In a café there are 8 tables with 5 chairs at each table. How many chairs are there altogether?	
7	What is the difference between 71 and 38?	
8	In the playground 56 children get into 7 equal lines. How many children are in each line?	
9	Find the answer to 69 add 45.	
10	Find one half of the answer to 6 multiplied by 3.	

1.1 Looking back (b)

Name ____________________

Date ____________________

		Answers
1	In three rounds of a game Rosie scores 17, 25 and 19 points. How many points does Rosie score altogether?	
2	What is 570 multiplied by 2?	
3	What number is half-way between 30 and 90?	
4	Calculate 80 added to 351.	
5	From 216 subtract 70.	
6	What is the cost of 3 rubbers at 17 pence each?	
7	What is one quarter of 72?	
8	Subtract 800 from 3000.	
9	Add 94 to 48.	
10	44 oranges are put into packs of 6. How many packs are made, and how many oranges are left over?	

1.1 Looking forward

Add two-digit and three-digit multiples of 10 and 100

• 70 add 40	*110*
• 300 add 900	*1200*
• 800 add 500	*1300*
• 60 add 60	*120*
• 90 add 20	*110*
• 600 add 700	*1300*

Split a two-digit or three-digit number in various ways

• 78 is 75 and what?	*3*
• 486 is 450 and what?	*36*
• 308 is 100 and what?	*208*
• 62 is 50 and what?	*12*
• 816 is 700 and what?	*116*
• 51 is 25 and what?	*26*

Add two-digit multiples of 10 to three-digit multiples of 100

• 70 add 400	*470*
• 500 add 30	*530*
• 600 add 90	*690*
• 10 add 800	*810*
• 300 add 20	*320*
• 200 add 50	*250*

Subtract two-digit multiples of 10 from three-digit multiples of 100

• 300 subtract 80	*220*
• 900 subtract 10	*890*
• 400 subtract 20	*380*
• 600 subtract 70	*530*
• 500 subtract 30	*470*
• 700 subtract 60	*640*

Multiply and divide a two-digit or three-digit number by 10

• 32 multiplied by 10	*320*
• 70 divided by 10	*7*
• 400 divided by 10	*40*
• 219 multiplied by 10	*2190*
• 520 divided by 10	*52*
• 99 multiplied by 10	*990*

Half of a two-digit multiple of 10 and a three-digit multiple of 100

• one half of 80	*40*
• one half of 300	*150*
• one half of 600	*300*
• one half of 90	*45*
• one half of 700	*350*
• one half of 40	*20*

1.2 Addition

Content

- addition of two three-digit multiples of 10
  (carrying to hundreds and possibly to thousands, answer less than 2000)

Helpful knowledge and skills

- be able to add two three-digit multiples of 100
- be able to add two two-digit multiples of 10
- be able to add a two-digit multiple of 10 to a three-digit multiple of 100
- be able to subtract a two-digit multiple of 10 from a three-digit multiple of 100

EXAMPLE

Find the sum of 370 and 580

STRATEGY **Near 400 and Near 600**

$370 + 580 = (400 - 30) + (600 - 20)$	• adjust to 400 and 600 and balance
$= (400 + 600) - 30 - 20$	• reorder and regroup
$= 1000 - 30 - 20$	• add
$= 970 - 20$	• subtract
$= 950$	• subtract

STRATEGY **Parts (hundreds and tens)**

$370 + 580 = (300 + 70) + (500 + 80)$	• split to hundreds and tens
$= (300 + 500) + (70 + 80)$	• reorder and regroup
$= 800 + 150$	• add
$= 950$	• add

STRATEGY **Parts (complement to 400)**

$370 + 580 = 370 + (30 + 550)$	• split to make up to 400
$= (370 + 30) + 550$	• regroup
$= 400 + 550$	• add
$= 950$	• add

SHARE AND DISCUSS

850 add 470

First I changed the 850 to 900 and the 470 to 500 and added them. Then I took away 80.

STRATEGY Near 900 and Near 500

1 What is 390 plus 430? *820*

2 Calculate 760 add 480. *1240*

3 Find the total of 650 and 670. *1320*

4 Add 920 to 890. *1810*

5 Find the answer to 570 add 740. *1310*

6 What is 880 add 850? *1730*

SHARE AND SYMBOLISE

Add 180 to 790

I added 80 to 90 to get 170 and then added 800. The answer is 970.

STRATEGY Parts (hundreds and tens)

$$
\begin{aligned}
180 + 790 &= 100 + 80 + 700 + 90 \\
&= 80 + 90 + 100 + 700 \\
&= 170 + 800 \\
&= 970
\end{aligned}
$$

1 What is the answer to 230 plus 680? *910*

2 Calculate 550 plus 560. *1110*

3 What is the sum of 480 and 980? *1460*

4 Find the sum of 890 and 770. *1660*

5 What is 160 add 890? *1050*

6 What is the total of 940 and 270? *1210*

PRACTISE AND DISCUSS

1 Find the total of 730 and 890. *1620*

2 Calculate 290 add 950. *1240*

3 Calculate 580 plus 560. *1140*

4 What is 340 plus 990? *1330*

5 What is the sum of 670 and 380? *1050*

6 What is 270 add 450? *720*

7 Find the answer to 190 add 790. *980*

8 What is 960 add 370? *1330*

9 Add 850 to 880. *1730*

10 What is the total of 780 and 640? *1420*

1.3 Subtraction

Content

- subtraction of a three-digit multiple of 10 from a three-digit multiple of 10 (answer greater than 100)

Helpful knowledge and skills

- know how to split a three-digit number in various ways
- be able to subtract a two-digit multiple of 10 from a three-digit multiple of 10

EXAMPLE

Subtract 290 from 570

STRATEGY Parts (hundreds and tens)

570 – 290 = (500 + 70) – 200 – 90	• split to hundreds and tens
= (500 – 200) + 70 – 90	• reorder and regroup
= 300 + 70 – 90	• subtract
= 370 – 90	• add
= 280	• subtract

STRATEGY Parts (isolate 270)

570 – 290 = (270 + 300) – 270 – 20	• split to isolate 270
= (270 – 270) + (300 – 20)	• reorder and regroup
= 280	• subtract

STRATEGY Near 300

570 – 290 = 570 – 300 + 10	• adjust to 300 and balance
= 270 + 10	• subtract
= 280	• add

SHARE AND DISCUSS

What is 810 take away 320?

I took 300 away from 800, then took away 10, leaving 490.

STRATEGY Parts (hundreds and tens)

1 Take 270 away from 430. 160

2 What is 440 minus 160? 280

3 Subtract 640 from 920. 280

4 What is the difference between 470 and 280? 190

5 What is 810 take away 480? 330

6 From 530 take 390 away. 140

SHARE AND SYMBOLISE

What is 650 minus 380?

650 is 300 and 350. Take away 350 and the sum is 300 minus 30, which is 270.

STRATEGY Parts (isolate 350)

$$650 - 380 = 300 + 350 - 350 - 30$$
$$= 300 - 30$$
$$= 270$$

1 Take 370 away from 840. 470

2 What is 920 minus 560? 360

3 Subtract 190 from 720. 530

4 What is the difference between 650 and 830? 180

5 What is 190 less than 350? 160

6 From 640 take 350 away. 290

PRACTISE AND DISCUSS

1 What is 560 minus 370? 190

2 Reduce 710 by 460. 250

3 Subtract 230 from 820. 590

4 What is 660 take away 180? 480

5 From 910 take 440 away. 470

6 Take 260 away from 830. 570

7 What is 520 minus 150? 370

8 Subtract 590 from 740. 150

9 What is 370 less than 650? 280

10 What is the difference between 410 and 150? 260

1.4 Investigating addition

COLLECT DATA

1 ☐ 0 + 1 ☐ 0 = 3 ☐ 0

Give two examples:

170 + 150 = 320
140 + 190 = 330

170 + 150 = 320	140 + 190 = 330	180 + 180 = 360
110 + 190 = 300	180 + 160 = 340	150 + 170 = 320
180 + 120 = 300	150 + 180 = 330	190 + 160 = 350

Record children's examples on the board and keep for next lesson.

SORT AND ORDER DATA

Put the examples from the last lesson ready on the board.

Draw the sorting grid on the board.

Sort and order the examples in the grid. Leave gaps where necessary.
(The examples above are shown in shaded boxes.)

Complete the grid.

Answer								
300	310	320	330	340	350	360	370	380
110 + 190	120 + 190	130 + 190	**140 + 190**	150 + 190	160 + 190	170 + 190	180 + 190	190 + 190
120 + 180	130 + 180	140 + 180	**150 + 180**	160 + 180	170 + 180	**180 + 180**	190 + 180	
130 + 170	140 + 170	**150 + 170**	160 + 170	170 + 170	180 + 170	190 + 170		
140 + 160	150 + 160	160 + 160	170 + 160	**180 + 160**	**190 + 160**			
150 + 150	160 + 150	**170 + 150**	180 + 150	190 + 150				
160 + 140	170 + 140	180 + 140	190 + 140					
170 + 130	180 + 130	190 + 130						
180 + 120	190 + 120							
190 + 110								

Keep the completed grid for the next lesson.

SEARCH FOR PATTERNS

Put the grid from the last lesson ready on the board.

Ask the children to describe a pattern in the table.

A response may be: 'The first numbers go up in tens and the second numbers go down in tens'.
List some additions in a column to help them see why this happens.

140 + 190 = 330
150 + 180 = 330
160 + 170 = 330
170 + 160 = 330
180 + 150 = 330
190 + 140 = 330

Why do the answers stay the same?

You may need to help them by asking:

- *In what ways are the additions different?* — The first numbers go up by 10 each time. The second numbers go down by 10 each time.
- *In what ways are the additions the same?* — The answers are the same.
- *Why do the answers stay the same?* — Adding 10 to one number and subtracting 10 from the other number keeps the answer to the addition the same.

1.4 Mathematics problem: Half-way between

Content

- how to approach 'half-way' questions

EXAMPLE

What number is half-way between 350 and 580? 465

2+3= Picture this:

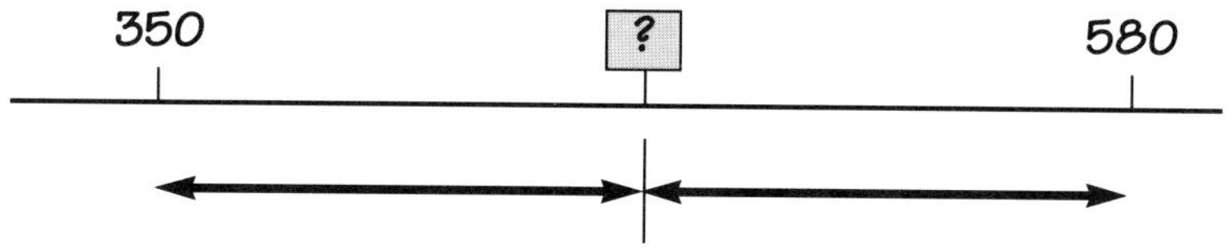

Add half the difference to the smaller number.

1. What is half-way between 185 and 395? 290
2. What is half-way between 850 and 420? 635
3. What is half-way between 406 and 512? 459
4. What is half-way between 532 and 764? 648
5. What is half-way between 140 and 980? 560
6. What is half-way between 358 and 564? 461

EXAMPLE

What number is half-way between 102 and 408? 255

2+3= Picture this:

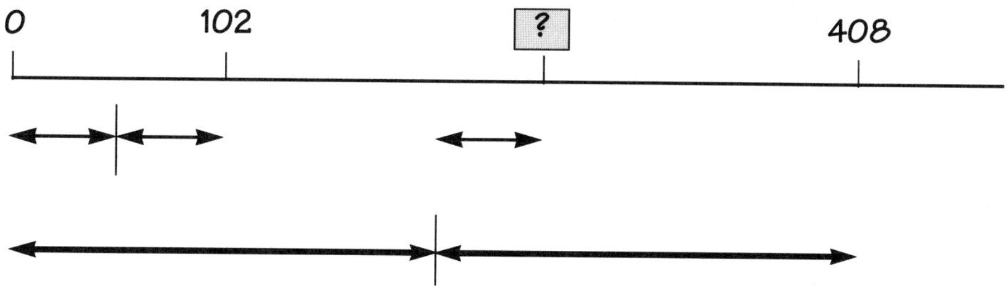

Add together half of each (or halve the sum of both).

1. What is half-way between 68 and 140? 104
2. What is half-way between 206 and 404? 305
3. What is half-way between 66 and 520? 293
4. What is half-way between 160 and 320? 240
5. What is half-way between 250 and 660? 455
6. What is half-way between 242 and 826? 534

1.5 Multiplication

Content

- multiplication of two two-digit multiples of 10

Helpful knowledge and skills

- know multiplication facts
- be able to multiply and divide by 10
- be able to take out a factor of 10

EXAMPLE

What is 40 multiplied by 60?

STRATEGY **Parts (factor of 10)**

$40 \times 60 = (4 \times 10) \times (6 \times 10)$	• split to isolate factors of 10
$= (4 \times 6) \times (10 \times 10)$	• reorder and regroup
$= 24 \times 100$	• use known facts
$= 2400$	• multiply

STRATEGY **Parts (factor of 10)**

$40 \times 60 = 40 \times (6 \times 10)$	• split to isolate factor of 10
$= (40 \times 6) \times 10$	• regroup
$= 240 \times 10$	• multiply
$= 2400$	• multiply

STRATEGY **Parts (factors)**

$40 \times 60 = 40 \times (10 \times 2 \times 3)$	• split to easier numbers
$= (40 \times 10) \times 2 \times 3$	• regroup
$= (400 \times 2) \times 3$	• multiply and regroup
$= 800 \times 3$	• multiply
$= 2400$	• multiply

SHARE AND DISCUSS

Multiply 80 and 90

> 8 times 9 equals 72, put on two noughts equals 7200.

STRATEGY Parts (factor of 10)

1 What is 90 times 40? 3600

2 Multiply 60 by 70. 4200

3 What is the answer to 80 times 20? 1600

4 Calculate 90 times 90. 8100

5 How much is 30 multiplied by 60? 1800

6 What is 80 multiplied by 60? 4800

SHARE AND SYMBOLISE

What is 70 times 30?

> I knocked the nought off and multiplied 70 by 3 which is 210. Then I put the nought back to make 2100.

STRATEGY Parts (factor of 10)

$$\begin{aligned} 70 \times 30 &= 70 \times (3 \times 10) \\ &= (70 \times 3) \times 10 \\ &= 210 \times 10 \\ &= 2100 \end{aligned}$$

1 Calculate 70 times 70. 4900

2 How much is 60 multiplied by 30? 1800

3 What is 90 multiplied by 60? 5400

4 What is 30 times 80? 2400

5 Multiply 40 by 70. 2800

6 What is the product of 60 and 20? 1200

PRACTISE AND DISCUSS

1 Calculate 60 multiplied by 80. 4800

2 What is 70 times 90? 6300

3 Multiply 80 by 40. 3200

4 What is the product of 90 and 30? 2700

5 How much is 60 times 60? 3600

6 Multiply 70 by 40. 2800

7 Calculate 80 times 30. 2400

8 How much is 90 multiplied by 20? 1800

9 What is 70 multiplied by 60? 4200

10 What is 80 times 80? 6400

1.6 Division

Content

- half and division by 2 of a three-digit number less than 200, with fractional answer

Helpful knowledge and skills

- be able to halve and divide by 2 a two-digit number
- be able to halve and divide by 2 a two-digit or three-digit multiple of 100
- know how to split a two-digit number in a variety of ways

EXAMPLE

Find one half of 162

STRATEGY Parts (hundreds, and tens and units)

$\frac{1}{2}$ of 162 = $\frac{1}{2}$ of (100 + 62)	• split to hundreds, and tens and units
= $\frac{1}{2}$ of 100 + $\frac{1}{2}$ of 62	• regroup (distributive law)
= 50 + 31	• halves
= 81	• add

EXAMPLE

Divide 137 by 2

STRATEGY Near 140

$137 \div 2 = (140 - 3) \div 2$	• adjust to 140 and balance
$= (140 \div 2) - (3 \div 2)$	• regroup (distributive law)
$= 70 - 1\frac{1}{2}$	• divide
$= 68\frac{1}{2}$	• subtract

STRATEGY Parts (hundreds, tens and units)

$137 \div 2 = (100 + 30 + 7) \div 2$	• split to hundreds, tens and units
$= (100 \div 2) + (30 \div 2) + (7 \div 2)$	• regroup (distributive law)
$= 50 + 15 + 3\frac{1}{2}$	• divide
$= 68\frac{1}{2}$	• add

SHARE AND DISCUSS

What is one half of 148?

> Half of 100 is 50, and 24 more is 74.

STRATEGY Parts (hundreds, and tens and units)

1. Find one half of 166. **83**
2. Share 108 equally into 2 parts. **54**
3. Find a half of 123. **$61\frac{1}{2}$**
4. What is 155 divided by 2? **$77\frac{1}{2}$**
5. Calculate 189 divided by 2. **$94\frac{1}{2}$**
6. Find 171 shared equally between 2. **$85\frac{1}{2}$**

SHARE AND SYMBOLISE

Divide 195 by 2

> 200 divided by 2 is 100. Take off $2\frac{1}{2}$ leaves $97\frac{1}{2}$.

STRATEGY Near 200

$$\begin{aligned}195 \div 2 &= (200 - 5) \div 2 \\ &= (200 \div 2) - (5 \div 2) \\ &= 100 - 2\tfrac{1}{2} \\ &= 97\tfrac{1}{2}\end{aligned}$$

1. Calculate 149 divided by 2. **$74\frac{1}{2}$**
2. What is one half of 187? **$93\frac{1}{2}$**
3. Halve 133. **$66\frac{1}{2}$**
4. What is 178 shared equally between 2? **89**
5. Share 129 into 2 equal parts. **$64\frac{1}{2}$**
6. Calculate 190 divided by 2. **95**

PRACTISE AND DISCUSS

1. Find 152 divided by 2. **76**
2. Divide 147 into 2 equal parts. **$73\frac{1}{2}$**
3. What is 193 divided by 2? **$96\frac{1}{2}$**
4. What is one half of 134? **67**
5. Halve 119. **$59\frac{1}{2}$**
6. Find a half of 135. **$67\frac{1}{2}$**
7. How many is one half of 184? **92**
8. Find 161 divided by 2. **$80\frac{1}{2}$**
9. What is 116 shared equally between 2? **58**
10. How many is one half of 177? **$88\frac{1}{2}$**

1.7 Investigating halving

COLLECT DATA

Put the diagram on the board. Start with multiples of 10.

The rule is: ***Stop halving when the units digit is a 5.***

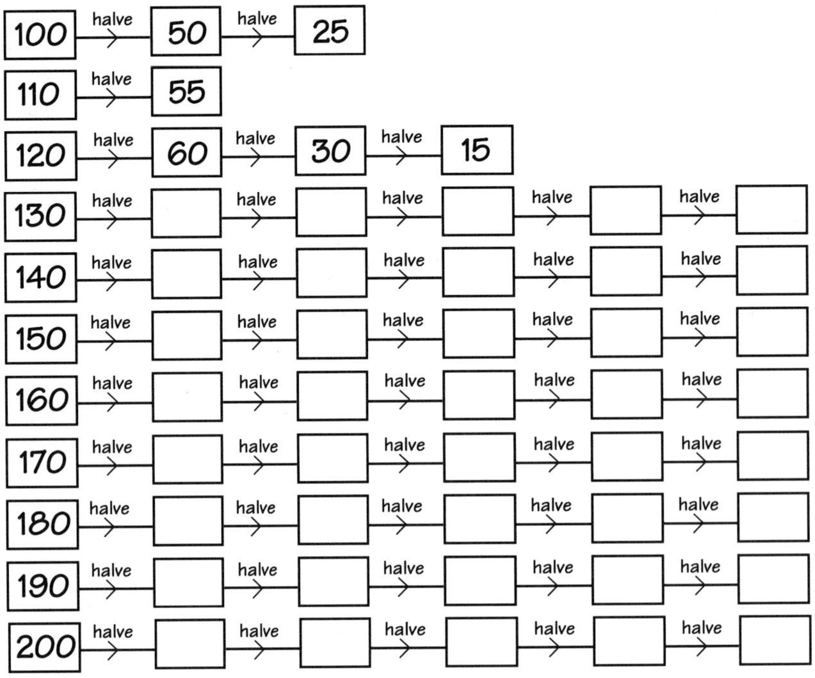

Record children's correct responses on the board. Keep them for the next lesson.

SORT, ORDER AND SEARCH FOR PATTERNS

Put the sequences from the last lesson ready on the board.

Draw the sorting grid on the board.

Sort and order the start numbers in the grid. Leave gaps where necessary. (The examples above are shown in shaded boxes.)

Put as many multiples of 10 in the grid as the time allows.

Number of times it is possible to halve a number						
1	2	3	4	5	6	7
110	100	120		160		
130	140	200				
150	180					
170						
190						

What do you notice about the numbers that can be halved only once?
What do you notice about the numbers that can be halved only twice?

Find a number that can be halved only 4 times.
Explain how you worked it out.
Find a number that can be halved only 6 times, only 7 times, … .

Simon's book has a mass of 730 grams. Sara's book has a mass of 580 grams. How many more grams is Simon's book than Sara's? *150 g*

2+3= Picture a balance:

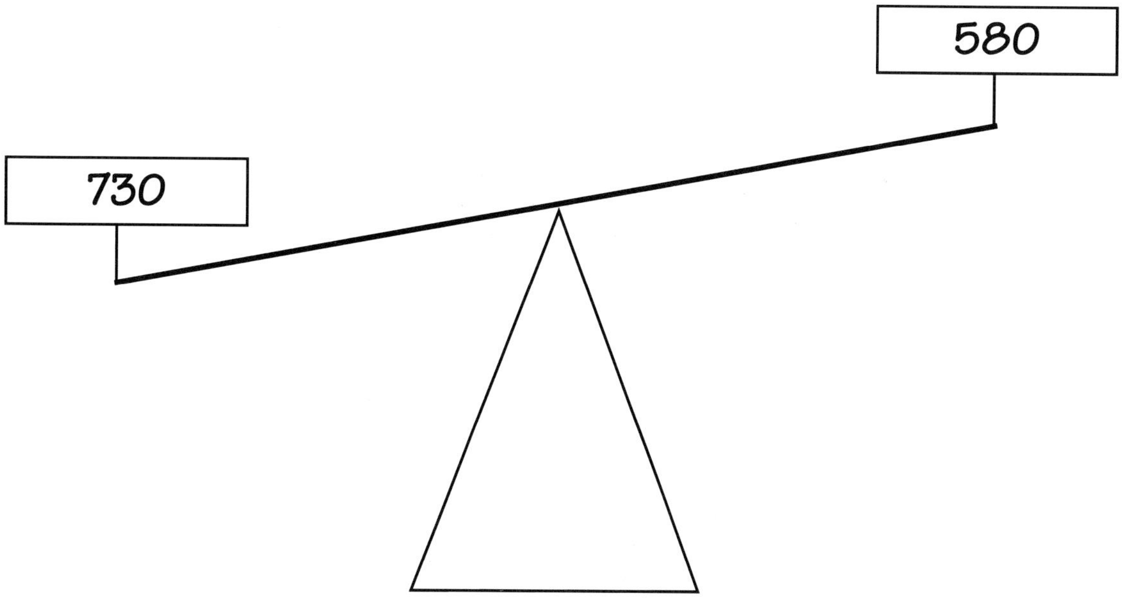

Think of the difference between the masses.

1 At a party, half of the balloons are red and half are blue. There are 176 balloons altogether. How many red balloons are there? *88*

2 Joe's yard backs onto Jane's yard. Joe's yard is 570 centimetres long and Jane's yard is 840 centimetres long. How long are their yards altogether? *1410 cm*

3 Pens cost 40 pence each. How much are 40 such pens? *£16*

4 The school library usually has 820 books. Penny counts 660 books on the shelves. How many books are being used? *160*

5 Rulers are 30 centimetres long. Carl collects 80 of them and lays them end to end in a straight line. How long is Carl's chain of rulers? *2400 cm*

6 Sandya has 146 marbles. She gives half of them to her sister. How many marbles does Sandya give to her sister? *73*

7 Paul's bedroom wall is 310 centimetres wide. His bed is 190 centimetres long. He puts his bed in the corner, along the wall. How long is the gap between the end of the bed and the wall? *120 cm*

8 A school has 340 girls and 370 boys. How many children are in the school altogether? *710*

1.8 Looking back (a)

Name ______________

Date ______________

		Answers
1	Add together 670 and 480.	
2	What is the cost of 20 pies at 90 pence each?	
3	What number is half-way between 260 and 410?	
4	What is 470 less than 620?	
5	Jackie has 154 stickers. She gives half of them away. How many does she have left?	
6	What is the sum of 260 and 590?	
7	What is half-way between 540 and 330?	
8	A room is 760 centimetres long. A carpet covers 390 centimetres of the length of the room, and the rest is tiled. How long is the tiled part of the room?	
9	Halve 162.	
10	Multiply 40 by 80.	

1.8 Looking back (b)

Name ______________

Date ______________

		Answers
1	Subtract 290 from 410.	
2	At a café, drinks are sold in three sizes. Small is 525 millilitres, large is 975 millilitres and medium is half-way between these. How many millilitres is a medium drink?	
3	What is the product of 70 and 60?	
4	Divide 172 by 2.	
5	A carpet covers 380 centimetres of the room length, and tiles cover the remaining 740 centimetres. What is the total length of the room?	
6	What number is half-way between 270 and 610?	
7	What is one half of 125?	
8	There are 80 pages in a pad of writing paper. How many pages are there altogether in 30 pads of writing paper?	
9	Calculate the sum of 890 and 950.	
10	What is the difference between 180 and 850?	

1.8 Looking forward

Add a three-digit multiple of 10 to a three-digit multiple of 100

- 380 add 800 | *1180*
- 700 add 920 | *1620*
- 410 add 600 | *1010*
- 100 add 990 | *1090*
- 540 add 800 | *1340*
- 900 add 270 | *1170*

Subtract a one-digit number from a three-digit multiple of 100

- 400 subtract 4 | *396*
- 700 subtract 8 | *692*
- 300 subtract 5 | *295*
- 900 subtract 2 | *898*
- 600 subtract 7 | *593*
- 200 subtract 9 | *191*

Divide using multiplication tables

- what multiplied by 6 is 24? | *4*
- what multiplied by 9 is 45? | *5*
- what multiplied by 3 is 27? | *9*
- what multiplied by 4 is 32? | *8*
- what multiplied by 7 is 49? | *7*
- what multiplied by 8 is 56? | *7*

Divide a two-digit multiple of 10 by a one-digit number (no remainder)

- divide 30 by 6 | *5*
- divide 90 by 9 | *10*
- divide 40 by 8 | *5*
- divide 20 by 4 | *5*
- divide 60 by 5 | *12*
- divide 60 by 3 | *20*

Subtract a two-digit number from a three-digit multiple of 100

- 400 subtract 37 | *363*
- 700 subtract 52 | *648*
- 600 subtract 48 | *552*
- 100 subtract 61 | *39*
- 900 subtract 85 | *815*
- 500 subtract 93 | *407*

Add a two-digit number to a three-digit multiple of 10

- 52 add 340 | *392*
- 61 add 230 | *291*
- 37 add 820 | *857*
- 24 add 450 | *474*
- 85 add 110 | *195*
- 43 add 630 | *673*

Content

- addition of a three-digit multiple of 10 to a two-digit number (carrying to hundreds, answer less than 1000)

Helpful knowledge and skills

- be able to add a two-digit or three-digit multiple of 10 to a three-digit multiple of 100
- be able to add two two-digit multiples of 10
- be able to subtract a one-digit number from a three-digit multiple of 100

EXAMPLE

Calculate the answer to 450 add 93

STRATEGY **Near 100**

450 + 93 = 450 + (100 − 7)	• adjust to 100 and balance
= (450 + 100) − 7	• regroup
= 550 − 7	• add
= 543	• subtract

STRATEGY **Parts (hundreds and tens) and Parts (tens and units)**

450 + 93 = (400 + 50) + (90 + 3)	• split to hundreds and tens, and split to tens and units
= 400 + (50 + 90) + 3	• regroup
= 400 + 140 + 3	• add
= 540 + 3	• add
= 543	• add

STRATEGY **Parts (complement to 500)**

450 + 93 = 450 + (50 + 43)	• split to make up to 500
= (450 + 50) + 43	• regroup
= 500 + 43	• add
= 543	• add

SHARE AND DISCUSS

What is the total of 59 and 190?

> I added 10 from the 59 onto the 190 to make 200, and then added the 49 to make 249.

STRATEGY Near 200

1 What is 53 add 460? 513

2 Calculate 790 add 76. 866

3 What is the sum of 41 and 180? 221

4 Add 680 and 54. 734

5 Find the total of 79 and 890. 969

6 Add 67 to 380. 447

SHARE AND SYMBOLISE

Find the sum of 370 and 63

> I added the 70 to 60 to make 130. Then I added the 3 making 133, and then 300 which made 433.

STRATEGY Parts (hundreds and tens) and Parts (tens and units)

$$\begin{aligned} 370 + 63 &= 300 + 70 + 60 + 3 \\ &= 300 + 130 + 3 \\ &= 300 + 133 \\ &= 433 \end{aligned}$$

1 Add together 92 and 240. 332

2 Find the answer to 570 add 45. 615

3 Calculate 58 add 380. 438

4 What is 64 plus 760? 824

5 Find the sum of 190 and 81. 271

6 What is 640 add 99? 739

PRACTISE AND DISCUSS

1 What is 33 add 580? 613

2 Calculate 470 add 72. 542

3 What is the sum of 85 and 260? 345

4 Add together 96 and 890. 986

5 Find the answer to 140 add 77. 217

6 Add 380 to 98. 478

7 Find the total of 69 and 750. 819

8 Add 650 to 94. 744

9 What is 71 add 260? 331

10 Find the sum of 880 and 85. 965

2.2 Subtraction

Content

- subtraction of a three-digit number from a four-digit multiple of 1000

Helpful knowledge and skills

- be able to subtract a two-digit number from a three-digit multiple of 100
- be able to subtract a three-digit multiple of 100 from a four-digit multiple of 1000

EXAMPLE

What is 3000 take away 572?

STRATEGY Near 600

3000 – 572	= (3000 – 600) + (600 – 572)	• subtract 600 and add 600 to balance
	= 2400 + 28	• subtract
	= 2428	• add

STRATEGY Parts (hundreds, and tens and units) and Parts (isolate a 100)

3000 – 572	= 3000 – 500 – 72	• split to hundreds, and tens and units
	= (3000 – 500) – 72	• regroup
	= 2500 – 72	• subtract
	= 2400 + (100 – 72)	• split to isolate a 100 and regroup
	= 2400 + 28	• subtract
	= 2428	• add

STRATEGY Parts (isolate 600)

3000 – 572	= (2400 + 600) – 572	• split to isolate 600
	= 2400 + (600 – 572)	• regroup
	= 2400 + 28	• subtract
	= 2428	• add

SHARE AND DISCUSS

What is 7000 subtract 498?

> I took away 500 from 7000 to make 6500. Then I took away 98 from 100 which made 2. So I added 2 to 6500 to make 6502.

STRATEGY **Near 500**

1 What is 3000 take away 274? 2726

2 Take 735 away from 6000. 5265

3 What is 814 less than 8000? 7186

4 What is the difference between 903 and 4000? 3097

5 What is 9000 minus 354? 8646

6 Subtract 548 from 2000. 1452

SHARE AND SYMBOLISE

Take 591 from 3000

> 500 from 3000 is 2500. 100 take away 91 is 9. So the answer is 2409.

STRATEGY **Parts (hundreds, and tens and units) and Parts (isolate a 100)**

$$
\begin{aligned}
3000 - 591 &= 3000 - 500 - 91 \\
&= 2500 - 91 \\
&= 2400 + (100 - 91) \\
&= 2409
\end{aligned}
$$

1 What is the difference between 369 and 5000? 4631

2 What is 4000 take away 511? 3489

3 From 7000 take 937 away. 6063

4 Take 556 away from 9000. 8444

5 What is 6000 minus 766? 5234

6 Subtract 384 from 8000. 7616

PRACTISE AND DISCUSS

1 Take 158 away from 2000. 1842

2 What is 5000 minus 493? 4507

3 Subtract 367 from 8000. 7633

4 What is 6000 take away 235? 5765

5 From 3000 take 423 away. 2577

6 What is the difference between 223 and 9000? 8777

7 What is 7000 minus 902? 6098

8 Subtract 654 from 4000. 3346

9 What is 6000 take away 582? 5418

10 What is 859 less than 5000? 4141

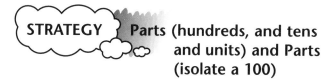

COLLECT DATA

2+3=

| 2 | 0 | 0 | 0 | – | | | 9 | = | | | | |

Give two examples:

2000 – 429 = 1571
2000 – 689 = 1311

2000 – 429 = 1571	2000 – 689 = 1311	2000 – 939 = 1061
2000 – 559 = 1441	2000 – 809 = 1191	2000 – 229 = 1771
2000 – 699 = 1301	2000 – 849 = 1151	2000 – 179 = 1821

Record children's examples on the board and keep for next lesson.

SORT AND ORDER DATA

2+3= Put the examples from the last lesson ready on the board.

Draw the sorting grid on the board.

Sort and order the examples in the grid by putting in the answers. Leave gaps where necessary. (The examples above are shown in shaded boxes.)

Complete the grid.

		Number of hundreds in the take-away number								
		1	2	3	4	5	6	7	8	9
Number of tens in the take-away number	0	1891	1791	1691	1591	1491	1391	1291	1191	1091
	1	1881	1781	1681	1581	1481	1381	1281	1181	1081
	2	1871	1771	1671	1571	1471	1371	1271	1171	1071
	3	1861	1761	1661	1561	1461	1361	1261	1161	1061
	4	1851	1751	1651	1551	1451	1351	1251	1151	1051
	5	1841	1741	1641	1541	1441	1341	1241	1141	1041
	6	1831	1731	1631	1531	1431	1331	1231	1131	1031
	7	1821	1721	1621	1521	1421	1321	1221	1121	1021
	8	1811	1711	1611	1511	1411	1311	1211	1111	1011
	9	1801	1701	1601	1501	1401	1301	1201	1101	1001

Keep the completed grid for the next lesson.

SEARCH FOR PATTERNS

2+3= Put the grid from the last lesson ready on the board.

Ask the children to describe a pattern in the table.

A response may be: 'All the answers start with 1 and end in 1'.
List some subtractions to help them see why this happens.

2000 – 409 = 1591
2000 – 419 = 1581
2000 – 429 = 1571
2000 – 439 = 1561
2000 – 449 = 1551

Why do the answers have a 1 in the thousands and a 1 in the units?

You may need to help them by asking:

- *How many thousands are there in the first number, and what is to be taken away?*
  There are 2 thousands in the first number, and taking away some hundreds will leave 1 thousand and some hundreds.
- *How many units are there in the first number, and how many units are to be taken away?*
  There are 0 units in the first number, and taking away 9 units means that 1 ten is needed from the tens. This leaves 9 units.

2.3 Mathematics problem: Measurements

Content

- conversion of measurement units

.... EXAMPLE ....

How many millimetres are there in 6.5 centimetres? *65 mm*

2+3= Picture the digits in their place value positions:

T	U	t
	6	5

x 10 →

T	U	t
6	5	

Shift the digits in the place value columns one to the left.

1 How many centimetres are there in 3.5 metres? *350 cm*

2 How many grams are there in 3.7 kilograms? *3700 g*

3 How many millilitres are there in 2.5 litres? *2500 ml*

4 How many centimetres are there in 350 millimetres? *35 cm*

5 How many metres are there in 260 centimetres? *2.6 m*

6 How many kilograms are there in 4300 grams? *4.3 kg*

.... EXAMPLE ....

How many minutes are there in $2\frac{1}{4}$ hours? *135 min*

2+3= Picture 60 minutes as the whole:

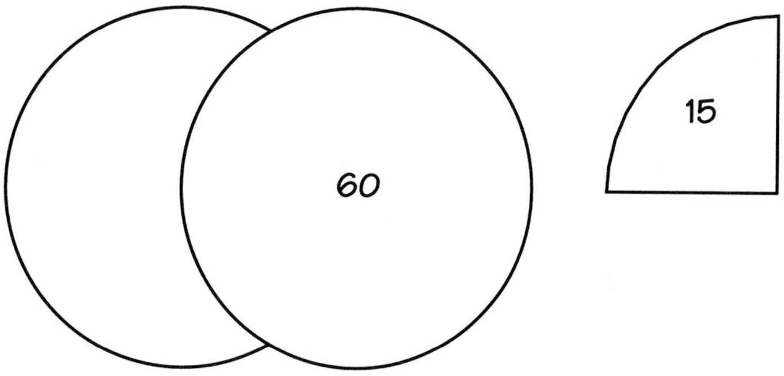

Separate wholes from parts.

1 How many seconds are there in 4 minutes? *240 s*

2 How many minutes are there in $5\frac{1}{2}$ hours? *330 min*

3 How many hours are there in 3 days? *72 h*

4 How many minutes are there in 210 seconds? *$3\frac{1}{2}$ min*

5 How many hours are there in 165 minutes? *$2\frac{3}{4}$ h*

6 How many days are there in 60 hours? *$2\frac{1}{2}$ days*

2.4 Multiplication

Content

- doubling a two-digit number

Helpful knowledge and skills

- know doubles of one-digit numbers
- be able to add a two-digit number less than 20 to a three-digit multiple of 10

EXAMPLE

Double 68

STRATEGY Parts (tens and units)

$68 \times 2 = (60 + 8) \times 2$	• split to tens and units
$= (60 \times 2) + (8 \times 2)$	• regroup (distributive law)
$= 120 + 16$	• multiply
$= 136$	• add

STRATEGY Near 70

$68 \times 2 = (70 - 2) \times 2$	• adjust to 70 and balance
$= (70 \times 2) - (2 \times 2)$	• regroup (distributive law)
$= 140 - 4$	• multiply
$= 136$	• subtract

STRATEGY Parts (known facts)

$68 \times 2 = (50 + 10 + 8) \times 2$	• split to easier numbers
$= (50 \times 2) + (10 \times 2) + (8 \times 2)$	• regroup (distributive law)
$= 100 + 20 + 16$	• multiply
$= 136$	• add

.... SHARE AND DISCUSS ....

Multiply 76 by 2

70 times 2 is 140, then 6 times 2 is 12, making 152.

STRATEGY Parts (tens and units)

1 Double 95. | 190

2 What is 57 multiplied by 2? | 114

3 What is 78 doubled? | 156

4 Calculate 99 times 2. | 198

5 What is twice 85? | 170

6 Multiply 56 by 2. | 112

.... SHARE AND SYMBOLISE ....

Calculate 59 times 2

59 is nearly 60, so I added 60 and 60 which made 120, then took away 2 to make 118.

STRATEGY Near 60

$$59 \times 2 = (60 \times 2) - (1 \times 2)$$
$$= 120 - 2$$
$$= 118$$

1 Calculate 98 times 2. | 196

2 What is twice 55? | 110

3 Multiply 77 by 2. | 154

4 Double 69. | 138

5 What is 88 multiplied by 2? | 176

6 What is 96 doubled? | 192

.... PRACTISE AND DISCUSS ....

1 Double 65. | 130

2 What is 97 multiplied by 2? | 194

3 What is 58 doubled? | 116

4 Calculate 67 times 2. | 134

5 What is twice 79? | 158

6 Calculate 86 times 2. | 172

7 What is twice 75? | 150

8 Multiply 89 by 2. | 178

9 Double 66. | 132

10 What is 87 multiplied by 2? | 174

2.5 Division

Content

- division of a two-digit number greater than 50 by a one-digit number, answer with no remainder (carrying to units)

Helpful knowledge and skills

- know how to split a two-digit number in a variety of ways
- be able to divide a two-digit multiple of 10 by a one-digit number, answer with no remainder
- be able to divide using knowledge of the simpler multiplication tables

EXAMPLE

Divide 87 by 3

STRATEGY Near 90

$87 \div 3 = (90 - 3) \div 3$	• adjust to 90 and balance
$= (90 \div 3) - (3 \div 3)$	• regroup (distributive law)
$= 30 - 1$	• divide
$= 29$	• subtract

STRATEGY Parts (known facts)

$87 \div 3 = (30 + 30 + 27) \div 3$	• split to easier numbers
$= (30 \div 3) + (30 \div 3) + (27 \div 3)$	• regroup (distributive law)
$= 10 + 10 + 9$	• use known facts
$= 29$	• add

STRATEGY Parts (known facts)

$87 \div 3 = (60 + 18 + 9) \div 3$	• split to easier numbers
$= (60 \div 3) + (18 \div 3) + (9 \div 3)$	• regroup (distributive law)
$= 20 + 6 + 3$	• divide
$= 29$	• add

SHARE AND DISCUSS

What is 76 divided by 4?

I added 4 on to 76 to make 80, which I divided by 4 to make 20. I then took 1 back, so the answer is 19.

STRATEGY Near 80

1. Find 84 divided by 6. *14*
2. Share 75 into 5 equal parts. *15*
3. Divide 54 into 3 equal parts. *18*
4. How many lots of 4 add up to 92? *23*
5. Calculate 72 divided by 3. *24*
6. What is 60 divided by 5? *12*

SHARE AND SYMBOLISE

Divide 91 by 7

I divided 70 by 7 which gave 10. This leaves 21, divided by 7 is 3. 10 add 3 gives 13.

STRATEGY Parts (known facts)

$$\begin{aligned} 91 \div 7 &= (70 + 21) \div 7 \\ &= (70 \div 7) + (21 \div 7) \\ &= 10 + 3 \\ &= 13 \end{aligned}$$

1. What is 84 shared equally between 3? *28*
2. Share 96 equally between 4. *24*
3. Share 84 into 7 equal parts. *12*
4. Share 42 into 3 equal parts. *14*
5. How many 6s are there in 96? *16*
6. What is 52 shared equally between 4? *13*

PRACTISE AND DISCUSS

1. Divide 85 by 5. *17*
2. Find 78 divided by 3. *26*
3. What is 96 divided by 8? *12*
4. Calculate 95 shared equally between 5. *19*
5. What is 68 divided by 4? *17*
6. How many 6s are there in 72? *12*
7. Find 87 divided by 3. *29*
8. Find 56 shared equally between 4. *14*
9. What is 45 shared equally between 3? *15*
10. Divide 90 by 6. *15*

2.6 Investigating doubling

COLLECT DATA

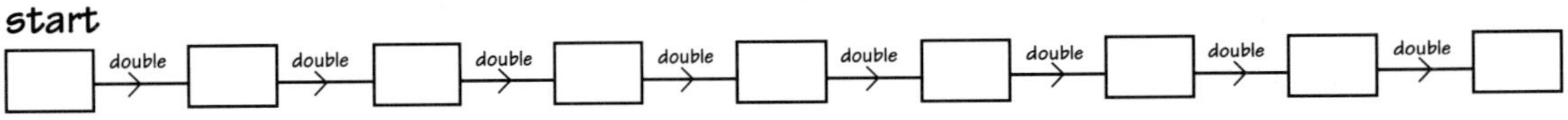

Give one example:

13 —double→ 26 —double→ 52 —double→ 104 —double→ 208 —double→ 416 —double→ 832 —double→ 1664 —double→ 3328

Record children's examples on the board and keep for next lesson.

21 —double→ 42 —double→ 84 —double→ 168 —double→ 336 —double→ 672 —double→ 1344 —double→ 2688 —double→ 5376

34 —double→ 68 —double→ 136 —double→ 272 —double→ 544 —double→ 1088 —double→ 2176 —double→ 4352 —double→ 8704

47 —double→ 94 —double→ 188 —double→ 376 —double→ 752 —double→ 1504 —double→ 3008 —double→ 6016 —double→ 12032

SEARCH FOR PATTERNS

Look for a pattern in the units digits.

You may need to help the children by underlining the units digits.

13 —double→ 26 —double→ 52 —double→ 104 —double→ 208 —double→ 416 —double→ 832 —double→ 1664 —double→ 3328

21 —double→ 42 —double→ 84 —double→ 168 —double→ 336 —double→ 672 —double→ 1344 —double→ 2688 —double→ 5376

34 —double→ 68 —double→ 136 —double→ 272 —double→ 544 —double→ 1088 —double→ 2176 —double→ 4352 —double→ 8704

47 —double→ 94 —double→ 188 —double→ 376 —double→ 752 —double→ 1504 —double→ 3008 —double→ 6016 —double→ 12032

The units digits in the first sequence go 3, 6, 2, 4, 8, 6, 2, 4, 8, … .
The units digits in the second sequence go 1, 2, 4, 8, 6, 2, 4, 8, 6, … .
The units digits in the third sequence go 4, 8, 6, 2, 4, 8, 6, 2, 4, … .
The units digits in the third sequence go 7, 4, 8, 6, 2, 4, 8, 6, 2, 4, … .

What is the pattern that is in all the sequences?
Will the pattern continue in each sequence?
Will the pattern appear whatever start number is used?
Test with other start numbers.

You may wish to show the children how the pattern in the units digits can be represented:

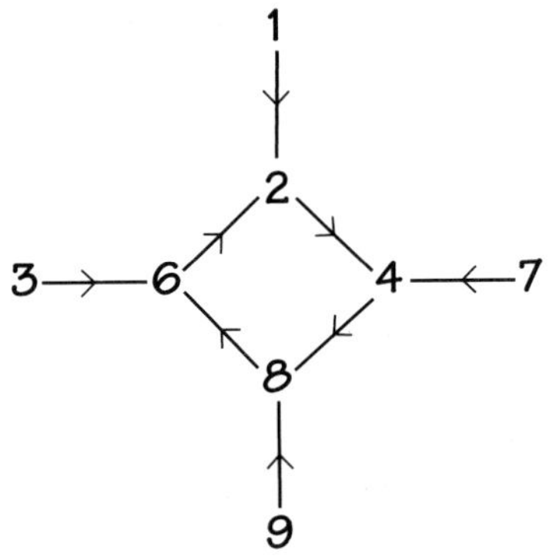

Ask the children to explain how this diagram works using one of their sequences.

What happens if the start number is 15 or 20?

2.6 Word problems

2 slices of bread are used to make a sandwich. How many slices of bread are needed to make 76 sandwiches? 152

Picture a sandwich and two slices:

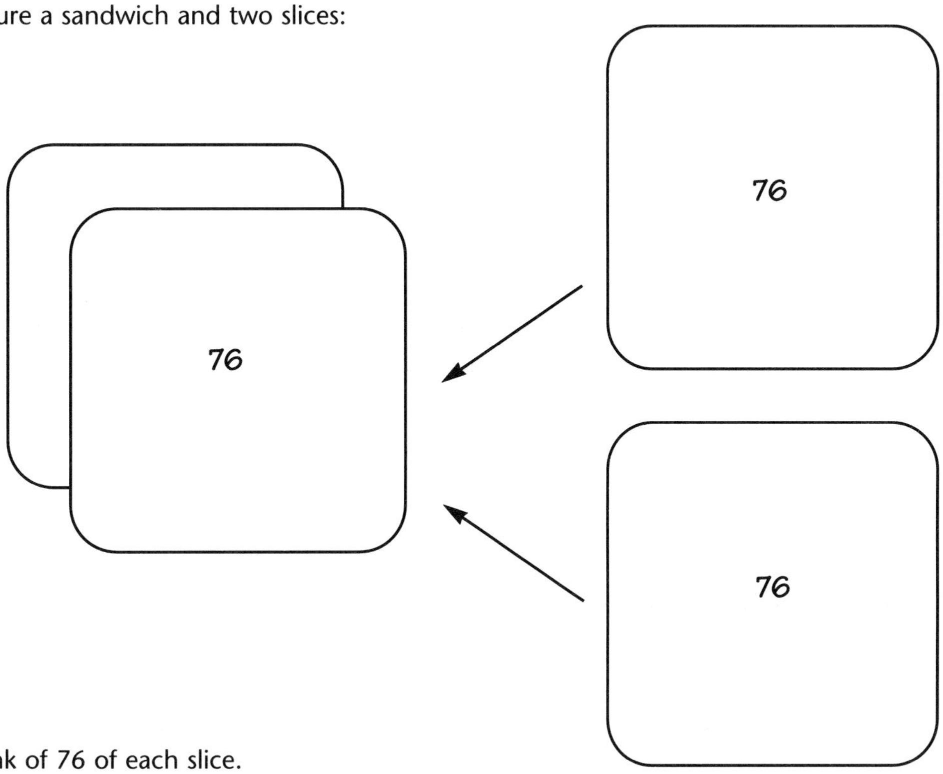

Think of 76 of each slice.

1. 42 eggs are put into egg boxes. Each egg box holds 6 eggs. How many boxes are used? 7
2. Toni has a collection of 470 stickers. She buys 47 more. How many stickers does she have now? 517
3. 3000 raffle tickets were on sale at a fête. At the end of the fête only 264 of the tickets were left. How many tickets were sold? 2736
4. At half-time, competitors are given half an orange each. 88 oranges are used. How many half-oranges are given out? 176
5. 56 felt-tip pens are shared equally among a group of 8 children. How many pens does each child get? 7
6. A church is trying to raise £5000 for a new roof. At the end of January it has raised £633. How much more does it need to raise? 4367
7. A tree in Helen's garden grew 38 centimetres in a year. At the beginning of the year it was 580 centimetres in height. How tall was it at the end of the year? 618 cm
8. In a survey, twice as many children liked bananas best as liked apples best. 97 children liked apples best. How many children liked bananas best? 194

2.7 Looking back (a)

Name ____________________

Date ____________________

		Answers
1	Double 66.	
2	Change 7.5 metres into centimetres.	
3	To 790 add 64.	
4	A gymnastics club is given a grant of £3000 to buy equipment. It decides to buy a small trampoline which costs £725. How much money is left?	
5	What is 60 divided by 4?	
6	What is 58 more than 270?	
7	Change 15 kilograms into grams.	
8	Subtract 384 from 6000.	
9	What is the cost of two melons at 87 pence each?	
10	What is 98 shared equally between 7?	

2.7 Looking back (b)

Name ____________________

Date ____________________

		Answers
1	How much is 192 less than 7000?	
2	Find twice 78.	
3	Write 55 millimetres in centimetres.	
4	Add 77 to 580.	
5	Dining tables seat 6 children. 78 children are to be seated. How many full tables will be needed?	
6	What is 4000 minus 851?	
7	On one day a museum is visited by 83 adults and 840 children. How many people in all visited the museum?	
8	What is 57 divided by 3?	
9	Change 3.5 litres into millilitres.	
10	What is double 59?	

2.7 Looking forward

Add two-digit multiples of 10 to three-digit numbers (without carrying)

- 324 add 50 *374*
- 70 add 516 *586*
- 40 add 739 *779*
- 428 add 60 *488*
- 177 add 20 *197*
- 80 add 612 *692*

Subtract a three-digit multiple of 100 from a three-digit number

- 756 subtract 300 *456*
- 415 subtract 100 *315*
- 674 subtract 200 *474*
- 583 subtract 400 *183*
- 967 subtract 600 *367*
- 892 subtract 700 *192*

Multiply a one-digit number by 5

- 7 multiplied by 5 *35*
- 4 multiplied by 5 *20*
- 8 multiplied by 5 *40*
- 2 multiplied by 5 *10*
- 6 multiplied by 5 *30*
- 9 multiplied by 5 *45*

Multiply a two-digit multiple of 10 by 5

- 30 multiplied by 5 *150*
- 50 multiplied by 5 *250*
- 60 multiplied by 5 *300*
- 90 multiplied by 5 *450*
- 40 multiplied by 5 *200*
- 70 multiplied by 5 *350*

Add two two-digit numbers

- 26 add 37 *63*
- 51 add 29 *80*
- 46 add 45 *91*
- 69 add 15 *84*
- 83 add 18 *101*
- 74 add 29 *103*

Subtract a one-digit number from a two-digit number

- 23 subtract 8 *15*
- 34 subtract 6 *28*
- 78 subtract 9 *69*
- 51 subtract 4 *47*
- 87 subtract 9 *78*
- 65 subtract 7 *58*

3.1 Addition

Content

- addition of three one-digit or two-digit numbers (carrying to tens, answer less than 100)

Helpful knowledge and skills

- be able to add two two-digit numbers
- be able to subtract a one-digit number from a two-digit number

EXAMPLE

Add 17, 29 and 34

STRATEGY Parts (known facts)

$17 + 29 + 34 = (15 + 2) + 29 + (35 - 1)$	• split and adjust to easier numbers and balance
$= (15 + 35) + 29 + (2 - 1)$	• reorder and regroup
$= 50 + 29 + 1$	• add and subtract
$= 80$	• add

STRATEGY Parts (tens and units)

$17 + 29 + 34 = (10 + 7) + (20 + 9) + (30 + 4)$	• split to tens and units
$= (10 + 20 + 30) + (7 + 9 + 4)$	• reorder and regroup
$= 60 + 20$	• add
$= 80$	• add

STRATEGY Near 30 and Near 35

$17 + 29 + 34 = 17 + (30 - 1) + (35 - 1)$	• adjust to 30 and 35 and balance
$= 17 + (30 + 35) - 2$	• reorder and regroup
$= (17 - 2) + 65$	• add, reorder and regroup
$= 15 + 65$	• subtract
$= 80$	• add

SHARE AND DISCUSS

Find the sum of 16, 24 and 40

> I turned 16 into 15 and put the 1 onto the 24 to make 25. Together they made 40, and 40 more is 80.

STRATEGY Parts (known fact)

1 What is 7 add 21 add 53? | 81
2 Calculate 45 add 24 add 9. | 78
3 Add 12, 45 and 26. | 83
4 Find the sum of 24, 31 and 18. | 73
5 What is 53 plus 4 plus 17? | 74
6 Find the total of 36, 23 and 15. | 74

SHARE AND SYMBOLISE

Calculate the total of 37 and 22 and 9

> I added the tens to get 50 and then added the units which was 18. I then added them together to make 68.

STRATEGY Parts (tens and units)

$$\begin{aligned} 37 + 22 + 9 &= 30 + 7 + 20 + 2 + 9 \\ &= 30 + 20 + 7 + 2 + 9 \\ &= 50 + 18 \\ &= 68 \end{aligned}$$

1 What is the answer to 13 add 6 add 72? | 91
2 Calculate 42 plus 32 plus 19. | 93
3 What is the sum of 12, 57 and 8? | 77
4 Add together 11, 16 and 44. | 71
5 Find the answer to 28 add 44 add 13. | 85
6 What is the answer to 3 plus 45 plus 49? | 97

PRACTISE AND DISCUSS

1 Add together 25 and 26 and 5. | 56
2 What is the sum of 17, 27 and 32? | 76
3 What is 29 plus 25 plus 14? | 68
4 Add 9 to 37 and add the answer to 45. | 91
5 What is the answer to 16 add 36 add 17? | 69
6 Calculate 38 add 29 add 12. | 79
7 Find the answer to 34 add 2 add 38. | 74
8 What is the answer to 49 plus 17 plus 30? | 96
9 Find the total of 11, 64 and 19. | 94
10 What is 53 add 28 add 16? | 97

3.2 Multiplication

Content

- multiplication of a two-digit number less than 20 by a one-digit number greater than 5

Helpful knowledge and skills

- know multiplication facts
- be able to add a two-digit number to a three-digit multiple of 10
- be able to subtract a two-digit number from a three-digit multiple of 10

EXAMPLE

Multiply 13 by 7

STRATEGY Parts (tens and units)

$13 \times 7 = (10 + 3) \times 7$	• split to tens and units
$= (10 \times 7) + (3 \times 7)$	• regroup (distributive law)
$= 70 + 21$	• multiply
$= 91$	• add

STRATEGY Near 10

$13 \times 7 = 13 \times (10 - 3)$	• adjust to 10 and balance
$= (13 \times 10) - (13 \times 3)$	• regroup (distributive law)
$= 130 - 39$	• multiply
$= 91$	• subtract

STRATEGY Parts (known facts)

$13 \times 7 = 13 \times (2 + 2 + 2 + 1)$	• split to easier numbers
$= (13 \times 2) + (13 \times 2) + (13 \times 2) + (13 \times 1)$	• regroup (distributive law)
$= 26 + 26 + 26 + 13$	• multiply
$= 52 + 26 + 13$	• add
$= 78 + 13$	• add
$= 91$	• add

SHARE AND DISCUSS

What is 16 multiplied by 8?

10 times 8 is 80. 6 times 8 is 48. Add them together makes 128.

STRATEGY Parts (tens and units)

1. Multiply 8 by 14. *112*
2. What is the answer to 19 times 6? *114*
3. How much is 16 multiplied by 7? *112*
4. What is the product of 9 and 18? *162*
5. What is 17 multiplied by 6? *102*
6. Calculate 8 times 15. *120*

SHARE AND SYMBOLISE

Calculate 14 multiplied by 9

9 is nearly 10, so 10 times 14 is 140, take 14 is 126.

STRATEGY Near 10

$$
\begin{aligned}
14 \times 9 &= 14 \times 10 - 14 \\
&= 140 - 14 \\
&= 126
\end{aligned}
$$

1. What is 17 times 9? *153*
2. Multiply 18 by 6. *108*
3. Calculate 12 times 8. *96*
4. What is the product of 7 and 14? *98*
5. How much is 19 multiplied by 9? *171*
6. Calculate 15 multiplied by 7. *105*

PRACTISE AND DISCUSS

1. Multiply 6 by 13. *78*
2. What is 7 times 12? *84*
3. Multiply 18 by 8. *144*
4. What is the answer to 14 times 6? *84*
5. Calculate 13 multiplied by 8. *104*
6. How much is 17 times 7? *119*
7. Calculate 15 times 6. *90*
8. How much is 12 multiplied by 9? *108*
9. What is 19 multiplied by 7? *133*
10. What is 9 times 13? *117*

3.3 Investigating multiplication

COLLECT DATA

1☐ × ☐ = 1☐☐

Give two examples:

17 × 6 = 102
14 × 9 = 126

17 × 6 = 102	14 × 9 = 126	16 × 8 = 128
13 × 8 = 104	19 × 6 = 114	15 × 7 = 105

Record children's examples on the board and keep for next lesson.

SORT AND ORDER DATA

Put the examples from the last lesson ready on the board.

Draw the sorting grid on the board.

Sort and order the examples in the grid. Leave gaps where necessary.
(The examples above are shown in shaded boxes.)

Complete the grid.

Answers should have three digits. The light diagonal shading shows answers with only two digits. These may be completed later.

Second number	First number 11	12	13	14	15	16	17	18	19
9		108	117	126	135	144	153	162	171
8			104	112	120	128	136	144	152
7					105	112	119	126	133
6							102	108	114
5									
4									
3									
2									
1									

Keep the completed grid for the next lesson.

SEARCH FOR PATTERNS

Put the grid from the last lesson ready on the board.

Ask the children to describe a pattern in the table.

A response may be: 'In the 19 column the units go up in ones'.
List the multiplications to help them see why this happens.

19 × 9 = 171
19 × 8 = 152
19 × 7 = 133
19 × 6 = 114

Why do the units go up in ones?

You may need to help them by asking:

- *In what ways are the multiplications different?* The second numbers go down in ones. The answers go down in 19s.
- *In what ways are the multiplications the same?* The first number is always 19.
- *Why do the units go up in ones?* Each answer is 19 less than the previous answer. This is the same as subtracting 20 (2 tens) and adding 1 (1 unit).

3.3 Mathematics problem: Rounding

Content

- rounding to the nearest whole number or multiple of 1000

EXAMPLE

What is 6.7 to the nearest whole number? 7

Picture a number line:

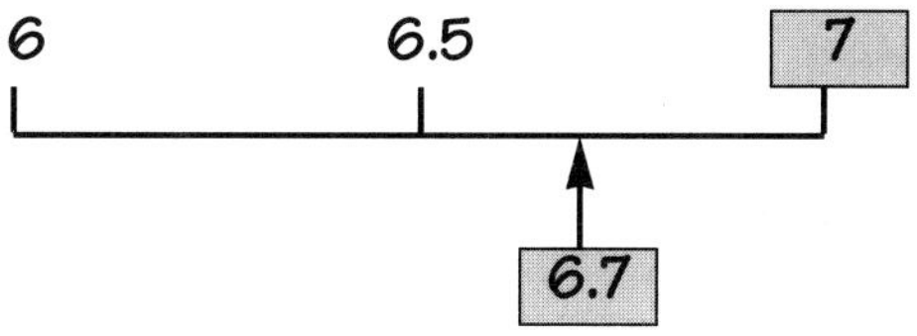

Think of the positions of the numbers.

1. What is 4.4 to the nearest whole number? 4
2. What is 2.48 to the nearest whole number? 2
3. What is 7.72 to the nearest whole number? 8
4. What is 6.04 to the nearest whole number? 6
5. What is 9.6 to the nearest whole number? 10
6. What is 39.48 to the nearest whole number? 39

EXAMPLE

What is 5387 to the nearest thousand? 5000

Picture this:

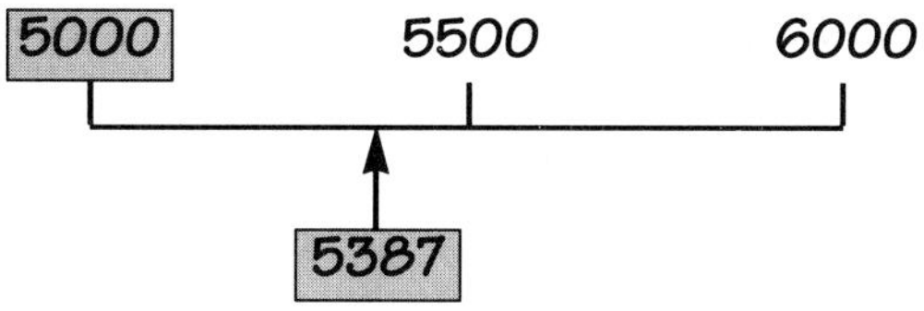

Think of the positions of the numbers.

1. What is 7444 to the nearest thousand? 7000
2. What is 9348 to the nearest thousand? 9000
3. What is 7512 to the nearest thousand? 8000
4. What is 6604 to the nearest thousand? 7000
5. What is 9659 to the nearest thousand? 10 000
6. What is 33 842 to the nearest thousand? 34 000

3.4 Subtraction

Content

- subtraction of a three-digit multiple of 10 from a three-digit number (answer greater than 100)

Helpful knowledge and skills

- be able to subtract a three-digit multiple of 100 from a three-digit number
- be able to add a two-digit multiple of 10 to a three-digit number

EXAMPLE

Subtract 450 from 812

STRATEGY Near 500

812 – 450 = 812 – 500 + 50	• adjust to 500 and balance
= (812 – 500) + 50	• group
= 312 + 50	• subtract
= 362	• add

STRATEGY Parts (hundreds, and tens and units)

812 – 450 = (800 + 12) – (400 + 50)	• split to hundreds, and tens and units
= (800 – 400) – 50 + 12	• reorder and regroup
= (400 – 50) + 12	• subtract and regroup
= 350 + 12	• subtract
= 362	• add

STRATEGY Near 500

812 – 450 = (812 + 50) – (450 + 50)	• adjust to 500 and balance
= 862 – 500	• add
= 362	• subtract

SHARE AND DISCUSS

What is 846 take away 290?

Take 300 away from 846 makes 546. Then add 10 to make 556.

STRATEGY Near 300

1 Take 270 away from 435. | 165 |

2 What is 448 minus 160? | 288 |

3 Subtract 640 from 924. | 284 |

4 What is the difference between 477 and 280? | 197 |

5 What is 480 less than 816? | 336 |

6 From 531 take 390 away. | 141 |

SHARE AND SYMBOLISE

What is 429 minus 130?

400 take away 100 is 300. 300 minus 1 is 299.

STRATEGY Parts (hundreds, and tens and units)

$$429 - 130 = (400 - 100) + (29 - 30)$$
$$= 300 - 1$$
$$= 299$$

1 Take 370 away from 842. | 472 |

2 What is 924 minus 560? | 364 |

3 Subtract 190 from 729. | 539 |

4 What is the difference between 650 and 837? | 187 |

5 What is 353 take away 190? | 163 |

6 From 645 take 350 away. | 295 |

PRACTISE AND DISCUSS

1 What is 568 minus 370? | 198 |

2 Reduce 716 by 460. | 256 |

3 What is 230 less than 823? | 593 |

4 What is 669 take away 180? | 489 |

5 From 911 take 440 away. | 471 |

6 Take 260 away from 834. | 574 |

7 What is 522 minus 150? | 372 |

8 Subtract 590 from 745. | 155 |

9 What is 659 take away 370? | 289 |

10 What is the difference between 417 and 150? | 267 |

Content

- multiplication of a two-digit number greater than 30 by 5 (carrying to tens and to hundreds)

Helpful knowledge and skills

- know 5 times table
- be able to multiply a two-digit multiple of 10 by 5

EXAMPLE

What is 89 multiplied by 5?

STRATEGY Parts (tens and units)

$89 \times 5 = (80 + 9) \times 5$	• split to tens and units
$= (80 \times 5) + (9 \times 5)$	• regroup (distributive law)
$= 400 + 45$	• multiply
$= 445$	• add

STRATEGY Parts (known facts)

$89 \times 5 = (20 + 20 + 20 + 20 + 9) \times 5$	• split to easier numbers
$= (20 \times 5) + (20 \times 5) + (20 \times 5) + (20 \times 5) + (9 \times 5)$	• regroup (distributive law)
$= 100 + 100 + 100 + 100 + 45$	• multiply
$= 445$	• add

STRATEGY Near 90

$89 \times 5 = (90 - 1) \times 5$	• adjust to 90 and balance
$= (90 \times 5) - (1 \times 5)$	• regroup (distributive law)
$= 450 - 5$	• multiply
$= 445$	• subtract

SHARE AND DISCUSS

Calculate 56 times 5

50 times 5 is 250.
6 times 5 is 30. Add them together gives 280.

STRATEGY **Parts (tens and units)**

1 Multiply 83 by 5. 415

2 What is the answer to 46 times 5? 230

3 Calculate 53 multiplied by 5. 265

4 How much is 75 multiplied by 5? 375

5 What is 69 multiplied by 5? 345

6 What is 5 times 94? 470

SHARE AND SYMBOLISE

What is 37 multiplied by 5?

I multiplied 20 by 5, then multiplied 10 by 5 and then 7 by 5. Add them up makes 185.

STRATEGY **Parts (known facts)**

$$\begin{aligned} 37 \times 5 &= (20 + 10 + 7) \times 5 \\ &= (20 \times 5) + (10 \times 5) + (7 \times 5) \\ &= 100 + 50 + 35 \\ &= 185 \end{aligned}$$

1 Multiply 5 by 87. 435

2 What is the product of 5 and 34? 170

3 Calculate 59 multiplied by 5. 295

4 How much is 96 times 5? 480

5 Calculate 48 times 5. 240

6 What is 85 multiplied by 5? 425

PRACTISE AND DISCUSS

1 What is 5 multiplied by 64? 320

2 Multiply 5 by 78. 390

3 What is 5 times 45? 225

4 Multiply 67 by 5. 335

5 Calculate 33 multiplied by 5. 165

6 How much is 57 times 5? 285

7 Calculate the product of 98 and 5. 490

8 How much is 39 multiplied by 5? 195

9 What is 66 multiplied by 5? 330

10 What is the answer to 74 times 5? 370

3.6 Investigating subtraction

COLLECT DATA

3□□ – 2□0 = □7

Give two examples:

327 – 280 = 47
357 – 260 = 97

327 – 280 = 47	357 – 260 = 97	307 – 250 = 57
387 – 290 = 97	367 – 280 = 87	327 – 250 = 77

Record children's examples on the board and keep for next lesson.

SORT AND ORDER DATA

Put the examples from the last lesson ready on the board.

Draw the sorting grid on the board.

Sort and order the examples in the grid. Leave gaps where necessary.
(The examples above are shown in shaded boxes.)

Complete the grid.

Answers should have two digits. The light diagonal shading shows answers with three digits.
These may be completed later.

Second number	First number								
	307	317	327	337	347	357	367	377	387
210	97								
220	87	97							
230	77	87	97						
240	67	77	87	97					
250	57	67	77	87	97				
260	47	57	67	77	87	97			
270	37	47	57	67	77	87	97		
280	27	37	47	57	67	77	87	97	
290	17	27	37	47	57	67	77	87	97

Keep the completed grid for the next lesson.

SEARCH FOR PATTERNS

Put the grid from the last lesson ready on the board.

Ask the children to describe a pattern in the table.

A response may be: 'The answers in a diagonal go down to the left in 20s'.
List some subtractions to help them see why this happens.

337 – 240 = 97
327 – 250 = 77
317 – 260 = 57
307 – 270 = 37

Why do the answers decrease by 20 each time?

You may need to help them by asking:

- *In what ways are the subtractions different?*
  The first numbers decrease by 10.
  The second numbers increase by 10.
  The answers decrease by 20.
- *Why do the answers decrease by 20?*
  Subtracting 10 more from a number which is 10 less means the answer will be 20 less.

3.6 Word problems

Tapes are sold in packs of 5. A school buys 28 packs. How many tapes does the school buy?

140

Picture a pack of 5 tapes:

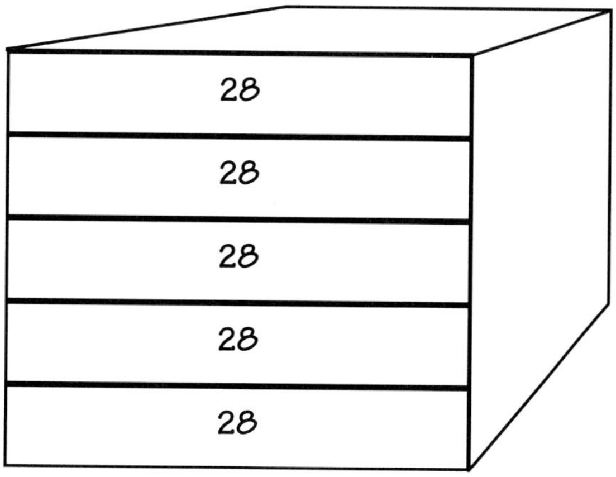

Think of 28 of each tape.

1 A pencil costs 28 pence, a ruler 33 pence and a rubber 24 pence. What is the total cost of all three? *85p*

2 A full bottle of milk has a mass of 765 grams. An empty bottle has a mass of 190 grams. What is the mass of the milk? *575 g*

3 There are 8 pens in a pack. How many pens are there in 16 packs? *128*

4 What is the value of 66 five-pence coins? *£3.30*

5 A computer that usually sells for £825 is on special offer, with £250 off the price. What is the special offer price? *£575*

6 The numbers of children in the three Year 5 classes are 34, 35 and 37. How many children are in Year 5? *106*

7 What is the total cost of 7 stamps at 19p each? *£1.33*

8 A school year consists of 39 weeks. There are 5 school days each week. How many school days are there in the school year? *195*

3.7 Looking back (a)

Name ____________________

Date ____________________

		Answers
1	Multiply 16 by 6.	
2	What is 7259 to the nearest thousand?	
3	In the three rounds of a game Nathan scores 27, 32 and 45. What is his total score?	
4	What is 821 subtract 260?	
5	Add together 41, 16 and 28.	
6	What is 5.8 to the nearest whole number?	
7	Calculate 65 times 5.	
8	Out of the 348 children in a school, 170 are girls. How many are boys?	
9	What is the product of 8 and 19?	
10	Multiply 86 by 5.	

3.7 Looking back (b)

Name ____________________

Date ____________________

		Answers
1	What is 54 plus 24 plus 14?	
2	Write 7.25 to the nearest whole number.	
3	What is 16 times 9?	
4	Subtract 390 from 478.	
5	One bus can seat 47 people. How many people can be seated on 5 such buses?	
6	Round 3503 to the nearest thousand.	
7	Sanjit buys a newspaper costing 26 pence, a comic costing 39 pence and a bar of chocolate costing 33 pence. How much is this altogether?	
8	What is 5 times 58?	
9	On his birthday John works out that there are exactly 18 weeks to Christmas. How many days are there in 18 weeks?	
10	What is the difference between 655 and 480?	

3.7 Looking forward

Double two-digit multiples of 10 and three-digit multiples of 100

- double 60 *120*
- double 300 *600*
- double 90 *180*
- double 70 *140*
- double 200 *400*
- double 400 *800*

Subtract a two-digit multiple of 10 from a four-digit multiple of 100

- 2300 subtract 50 *2250*
- 7600 subtract 20 *7580*
- 8100 subtract 40 *8060*
- 4500 subtract 70 *4430*
- 6400 subtract 90 *6310*
- 1900 subtract 60 *1840*

Add a one-digit number to a three-digit number

- 328 add 9 *337*
- 7 add 444 *451*
- 6 add 835 *841*
- 666 add 7 *673*
- 319 add 3 *322*
- 594 add 8 *602*

Add a two-digit multiple of 10 to a three-digit number

- 80 add 551 *631*
- 472 add 60 *532*
- 90 add 137 *227*
- 50 add 673 *723*
- 289 add 40 *329*
- 899 add 70 *969*

Divide a two-digit multiple of 10 by 5

- 80 divided by 5 *16*
- 30 divided by 5 *6*
- 90 divided by 5 *18*
- 20 divided by 5 *4*
- 60 divided by 5 *12*
- 70 divided by 5 *14*

Divide a three-digit multiple of 100 by 5

- 500 divided by 5 *100*
- 800 divided by 5 *160*
- 400 divided by 5 *80*
- 600 divided by 5 *120*
- 900 divided by 5 *180*
- 300 divided by 5 *60*

4.1 Division

Content

- division of a three-digit multiple of 5 by 5

Helpful knowledge and skills

- know how to split a three-digit number in a variety of ways
- be able to divide a two-digit or three-digit multiple of 10 by 5
- be able to divide a three-digit multiple of 100 by 5

EXAMPLE

Divide 290 by 5

STRATEGY Parts (known facts)

$290 \div 5 = (100 + 100 + 50 + 40) \div 5$ • split to easier numbers

$= (100 \div 5) + (100 \div 5) + (50 \div 5) + (40 \div 5)$ • regroup (distributive law)

$= 20 + 20 + 10 + 8$ • divide

$= 58$ • add

STRATEGY Parts (known facts) and Parts (factor of 10)

$290 \div 5 = \{(20 \times 10) + 90\} \div 5$ • split and take out factor of 10

$= (20 \times 10 \div 5) + (90 \div 5)$ • regroup (distributive law)

$= (20 \div 5 \times 10) + (90 \div 5)$ • reorder

$= 40 + 18$ • divide and multiply

$= 58$ • add

STRATEGY Near 300

$290 \div 5 = (300 - 10) \div 5$ • adjust to 300 and balance

$= (300 \div 5) - (10 \div 5)$ • regroup (distributive law)

$= 60 - 2$ • divide

$= 58$ • subtract

SHARE AND DISCUSS

What is 280 divided by 5?

> I took 30 away from the 80, leaving 50.
> 50 divided by 5 is 10 and 30 divided by 5 is 6.
> That's 16. 5 into 100 is 20, multiplied by 2 is 40.
> I added 16 and 40 to make 56.

STRATEGY **Parts (known facts)**

1. Find 340 divided by 5. *68*
2. Calculate 530 shared equally between 5. *106*
3. What is 160 divided by 5? *32*
4. Find 570 divided by 5. *114*
5. How many is 320 shared equally between 5? *64*
6. Share 450 into 5 equal parts. *90*

SHARE AND SYMBOLISE

Divide 135 by 5

> 10 times 5 is 50, twice 50 is 100,
> so 5 into 100 is 20. 5 times 7 is
> 35, add 20 and 7 makes 27.

STRATEGY **Parts (known facts) and Double**

$$135 \div 5 = (50 + 50 + 35) \div 5$$

$$= (50 \div 5) + (50 \div 5) + (35 \div 5)$$

$$= 10 \times 2 + 7$$

$$= 27$$

1. What is 225 shared equally between 5? *45*
2. What is 385 divided by 5? *77*
3. Divide 545 into 5 equal parts. *109*
4. Find the answer to 495 divided by 5. *99*
5. Divide 535 by 5. *107*
6. Calculate 665 divided by 5. *133*

PRACTISE AND DISCUSS

1. Share 130 into 5 equal parts. *26*
2. Find 750 divided by 5. *150*
3. What is 655 divided by 5? *131*
4. Share 270 into 5 equal parts. *54*
5. Divide 995 by 5. *199*
6. What is 115 shared equally between 5? *23*
7. Calculate 565 divided by 5. *113*
8. Find 440 shared into 5 equal parts. *88*
9. Calculate 425 divided by 5. *85*
10. Divide 730 by 5. *146*

4.2 Addition

Content

- addition of a two-digit number to a three-digit number (carrying to either tens or hundreds)

Helpful knowledge and skills

- be able to add a two-digit multiple of 10 to a three-digit number
- be able to add a one-digit number to a three-digit number
- be able to subtract a one-digit number from a two-digit number

EXAMPLE

What is 495 add 68?

STRATEGY Parts (tens and units)

495 + 68 = 495 + (60 + 8)	• split to tens and units
= (495 + 60) + 8	• regroup
= 555 + 8	• add
= 563	• add

STRATEGY Near 500

495 + 68 = (495 + 5) + 68 – 5	• adjust to 500 and balance
= 500 + 63	• add and subtract
= 563	• add

STRATEGY Near 70

495 + 68 = 495 + (70 – 2)	• adjust to 70 and balance
= (495 + 70) – 2	• regroup
= 565 – 2	• add
= 563	• subtract

SHARE AND DISCUSS

Add 375 to 17

I added 10 on to 375 and then added the 7, making 392.

STRATEGY Parts (tens and units)

1. Calculate 461 plus 85. *546*
2. What is the sum of 34 and 738? *772*
3. Calculate 27 add 153. *180*
4. Add 893 to 62. *955*
5. What is 345 add 29? *374*
6. Find the answer to 19 add 646. *665*

SHARE AND SYMBOLISE

Find the answer to 74 plus 284

I changed 284 to 300 and added 74 and then subtracted 16 to get 358.

STRATEGY Near 300

$$
\begin{aligned}
74 + 284 &= 74 + 300 - 16 \\
&= 374 - 16 \\
&= 358
\end{aligned}
$$

1. What is the answer to 22 plus 287? *309*
2. Find the total of 56 and 738. *794*
3. What is the answer to 428 add 14? *442*
4. What is 41 plus 949? *990*
5. Find the sum of 674 and 74. *748*
6. Add together 58 and 323. *381*

PRACTISE AND DISCUSS

1. What is the sum of 81 and 593? *674*
2. What is the answer to 325 plus 26? *351*
3. Calculate 237 add 72. *309*
4. Find the total of 946 and 35. *981*
5. Calculate 34 plus 117. *151*
6. What is 59 add 729? *788*
7. What is 427 plus 47? *474*
8. Find the answer to 65 add 674. *739*
9. Find the sum of 813 and 78. *891*
10. Add 62 to 266. *328*

4.3 Investigating division

COLLECT DATA

2+3=

Use the same start number for all three.

$\square\square 0 \div 5 = \square\square$

$\square\square 0 \div 10 \times 2 = \square\square$

$\square\square 0 \times 2 \div 10 = \square\square$

Give one example:

$320 \div 5 = 64$
$320 \div 10 \times 2 = 64$
$320 \times 2 \div 10 = 64$

Record children's examples.

$320 \div 5 = 64$	$450 \div 5 = 90$	$190 \div 5 = 38$
$320 \div 10 \times 2 = 64$	$450 \div 10 \times 2 = 90$	$190 \div 10 \times 2 = 38$
$320 \times 2 \div 10 = 64$	$450 \times 2 \div 10 = 90$	$190 \times 2 \div 10 = 38$

Ask the children to describe what they see.

Will it always work?
Try with more examples.

- *Why does it work?*

10 divided by 2 is 5. So dividing by 10 and then multiplying by 2 is the same as dividing by 5.

COLLECT DATA

2+3=

Use the same start number for all three.

$\square\square 5 \div 5 = \square\square$

$\square\square 5 \div 10 \times 2 = \square\square$

$\square\square 5 \times 2 \div 10 = \square\square$

Give one example:

$145 \div 5 = 29$		
$145 \div 10 = 14\frac{1}{2}$	$14\frac{1}{2} \times 2 = 29$	so $145 \div 10 \times 2 = 29$
$145 \times 2 = 290$	$290 \div 10 = 29$	so $145 \times 2 \div 10 = 29$

Record children's examples.

$435 \div 5 = 87$		
$435 \div 10 = 43\frac{1}{2}$	$43\frac{1}{2} \times 2 = 87$	so $435 \div 10 \times 2 = 87$
$435 \times 2 = 870$	$870 \div 10 = 87$	so $435 \times 2 \div 10 = 87$
$225 \div 5 = 45$		
$225 \div 10 = 22\frac{1}{2}$	$22\frac{1}{2} \times 2 = 45$	so $225 \div 10 \times 2 = 45$
$225 \times 2 = 450$	$450 \div 10 = 45$	so $225 \times 2 \div 10 = 45$

Ask the children to describe what they see.

Will it always work?
Try with more examples.

- *Why does it work?*

10 divided by 2 is 5. So dividing by 10 and then multiplying by 2 is the same as dividing by 5. Multiplying by 2 and dividing by 10 is the same as dividing by 5.

4.3 Mathematics problem: Time calculations

Content

- what to do with time calculations

EXAMPLE

What is the time 20 minutes after 9.50? *10.10*

2+3= Picture a clock face:

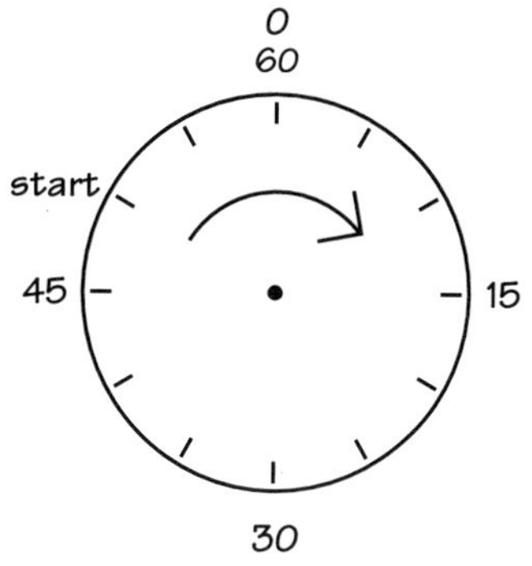

Count round in fives.

1 What time is it 15 minutes after 20 past 5? *5.35*

2 What time is it 50 minutes later than 3.30? *4.20*

3 Add 25 minutes to a time of 9.55. *10.20*

4 What is the time 35 minutes before quarter-past 11? *10.40*

5 A clock showing a time of five to 4 is 15 minutes fast. What is the correct time? *3.40*

6 What is the time that is 50 minutes earlier than half-past 7? *6.40*

EXAMPLE

How long is it from half-past 4 to a quarter to 6? *75 min*

2+3= Picture a clock face:

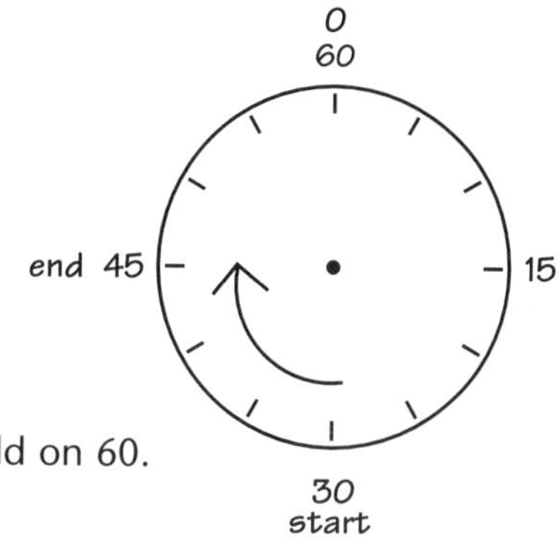

Count round in fives, then add on 60.

1 How long is it from quarter-to 3 to quarter-past 4? *90 min*

2 How long after five past 1 is five to 2? *50 min*

3 How many minutes are there between the times of 3.40 and 5.20? *100 min*

4 A programme due to start at 4.50 did not start until 6.10. How long was the delay? *80 min*

5 What is the duration of the time period between 8.25 and 10 o'clock? *95 min*

6 How long before 6.15 is half-past 3? *2 h 45 min*

4.4 Subtraction

Content

- subtraction of (i) a one-digit number from a four-digit multiple of 100, and (ii) a two-digit multiple of 10 from a four-digit multiple of 100

Helpful knowledge and skills

- be able to subtract a one-digit number from a three-digit multiple of 100
- be able to subtract a two-digit multiple of 10 from a three-digit multiple of 100

.... **EXAMPLE** ....

What is 40 less than 4500?

STRATEGY **Parts (isolate a 100)**

4500 – 40 = (4400 + 100) – 40	• split to isolate a 100
= 4400 + (100 – 40)	• regroup
= 4400 + 60	• subtract
= 4460	• add

STRATEGY **Parts (thousands and hundreds)**

4500 – 40 = (4000 + 500) – 40	• split to thousands and hundreds
= 4000 + (500 – 40)	• regroup
= 4000 + 460	• subtract
= 4460	• add

.... **EXAMPLE** ....

Calculate 1700 subtract 6

STRATEGY **Parts (isolate a 10)**

1700 – 6 = (1690 + 10) – 6	• split to isolate a 10
= 1690 + (10 – 6)	• regroup
= 1690 + 4	• subtract
= 1694	• add

SHARE AND DISCUSS

What is 1400 take away 60?

I took away 60 from 100, then added on the 1300 making 1340.

STRATEGY Parts (isolate a 100)

1 Subtract 70 from 6600. *6530*

2 What is 7200 take away 90? *7110*

3 What is 20 less than 3100? *3080*

4 Take 50 away from 9100. *9050*

5 What is 5400 minus 90? *5310*

6 Subtract 10 from 4900. *4890*

SHARE AND SYMBOLISE

What is 3600 minus 8?

I took away 8 from 600 which made 592. Then I added the 3000 to make 3592.

STRATEGY Parts (thousands and hundreds)

$$\begin{aligned} 3600 - 8 &= (3000 + 600) - 8 \\ &= 3000 + (600 - 8) \\ &= 3000 + 592 \\ &= 3592 \end{aligned}$$

1 Subtract 6 from 2600. *2594*

2 What is 9600 take away 3? *9597*

3 Reduce 8500 by 5. *8495*

4 What is 2800 minus 3? *2797*

5 What is the difference between 7700 and 8? *7692*

6 What is 5 subtracted from 4300? *4295*

PRACTISE AND DISCUSS

1 What is 6200 minus 40? *6160*

2 What is the difference between 3900 and 60? *3840*

3 Subtract 8 from 7400. *7392*

4 What is 9300 take away 6? *9294*

5 From 3600 take 20 away. *3580*

6 Take 4 away from 8800. *8796*

7 What is 2300 minus 30? *2270*

8 Subtract 7 from 8300. *8293*

9 What is 5200 take away 80? *5120*

10 What is 2 less than 5700? *5698*

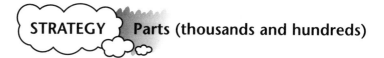

4.5 Multiplication

Content

- doubling a three-digit multiple of 10

Helpful knowledge and skills

- be able to double a two-digit multiple of 10
- be able to double a three-digit multiple of 100
- be able to subtract a two-digit multiple of 10 from a four-digit multiple of 100
- be able to add a two-digit or three-digit multiple of 10 to a four-digit multiple of 100

EXAMPLE

Double 780

STRATEGY Parts (hundreds and tens)

$780 \times 2 = (700 + 80) \times 2$	• split to hundreds and tens
$= (700 \times 2) + (80 \times 2)$	• regroup (distributive law)
$= 1400 + 160$	• multiply
$= 1560$	• add

STRATEGY Near 800

$780 \times 2 = (800 - 20) \times 2$	• adjust to 800 and balance
$= (800 \times 2) - (20 \times 2)$	• regroup (distributive law)
$= 1600 - 40$	• multiply
$= 1560$	• subtract

STRATEGY Parts (known fact)

$780 \times 2 = (750 + 30) \times 2$	• split to easier numbers
$= (750 \times 2) + (30 \times 2)$	• regroup (distributive law)
$= 1500 + 60$	• multiply
$= 1560$	• add

SHARE AND DISCUSS

What is 870 multiplied by 2?

First I doubled 70, which is 140.
Then I doubled 800, which is 1600.
I added them together and made 1740.

STRATEGY Parts (hundreds and tens)

1 Double 650. 1300

2 What is 580 doubled? 1160

3 Calculate 970 times 2. 1940

4 What is twice 750? 1500

5 Multiply 690 by 2. 1380

6 What is 880 multiplied by 2? 1760

SHARE AND SYMBOLISE

What is twice 590?

I would round it up to 600.
Twice 600 equals 1200, then take
the 20 away equals 1180.

STRATEGY Near 600

$$590 \times 2 = 600 \times 2 - 10 \times 2$$
$$= 1200 - 20$$
$$= 1180$$

1 What is 980 multiplied by 2? 1960

2 What is 550 doubled? 1100

3 What is twice 790? 1580

4 Calculate 860 times 2. 1720

5 Multiply 990 by 2. 1980

6 Double 680. 1360

PRACTISE AND DISCUSS

1 Double 560. 1120

2 What is 950 multiplied by 2? 1900

3 What is 670 doubled? 1340

4 Calculate 890 times 2. 1780

5 What is twice 760? 1520

6 Calculate 850 times 2. 1700

7 What is twice 570? 1140

8 Multiply 660 by 2. 1320

9 Double 960. 1920

10 What is 770 multiplied by 2? 1540

4.6 Investigating subtraction

COLLECT DATA

2+3=

1		0	0	–		=				

Give two examples:

1400 – 7 = 1393
1800 – 4 = 1796

1400 – 7 = 1393	1800 – 4 = 1796	1300 – 8 = 1292
1200 – 5 = 1195	1700 – 1 = 1699	1400 – 5 = 1395

Record children's examples on the board and keep for next lesson.

SEARCH FOR PATTERNS

2+3= Put the examples from the last lesson ready on the board.

Ask the children to describe a pattern in the answers.

A response may be: 'The answers always have 9 tens'.

List some subtractions to help them see this.

Why do the answers always have a 9 in the tens place?

1400 – 7 = 1393
1200 – 5 = 1195
1800 – 4 = 1796
1700 – 1 = 1699

You may need to help them by asking:

- *In what ways are the subtractions the same?*
- *Why do the answers always have a 9 in the tens place?*

The first numbers have no tens and no units.
The second numbers are single digits.
The answers always have a 9 in the tens place.
Take two examples to show the digit subtracted from a 100:
1400 – 7 = 1300 + 100 – 7 = 1300 + 93 = 1393
1200 – 5 = 1100 + 100 – 5 = 1100 + 95 = 1195

COLLECT DATA

2+3=

1		0	0	–		0	=				

Give two examples:

1900 – 30 = 1870
1300 – 40 = 1360

1900 – 30 = 1870	1300 – 40 = 1260	1500 – 80 = 1420
1200 – 40 = 1160	1700 – 90 = 1610	1400 – 50 = 1350

Record children's examples on the board and keep for next lesson.

SEARCH FOR PATTERNS

2+3= Put the examples from the last lesson ready on the board.

Ask the children to describe a pattern in the subtractions.

A response may be: 'The hundreds differ by 1'.

List some subtractions to help them see this.

Why do the hundreds always differ by 1?

1900 – 30 = 1870
1300 – 40 = 1260
1500 – 80 = 1420
1200 – 40 = 1160

You may need to help them by asking:

- *In what ways are the subtractions the same?*
- *Why do the hundreds always differ by 1?*

The first numbers have no tens and no units.
The second numbers are multiples of 10.
Take two examples to show the tens subtracted from a 100:
1900 – 30 = 1800 + 100 – 30 = 1800 + 70 = 1870
1300 – 40 = 1200 + 100 – 40 = 1200 + 60 = 1260

4.6 Word problems

A school is selling raffle tickets. Out of 2400 being sold there are only 90 left. How many have been sold? 2310

Picture the 2400 as a whole:

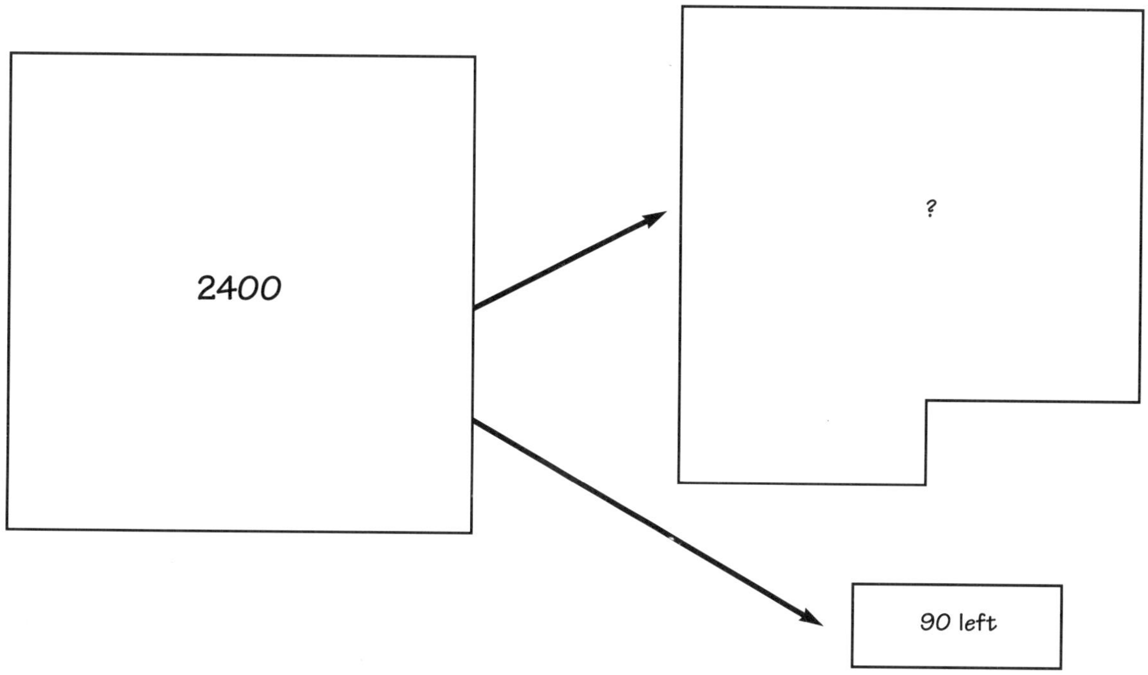

Split into '90' and 'the rest'.

1. A holiday to Russia costs £780 for each person.
   How much would it be for 2 people? *£1560*
2. In a tournament 135 children are put into teams of 5.
   How many teams are there? *27*
3. A book which has a mass of 385 grams is wrapped up as a parcel.
   The wrapping paper used has a mass of 38 grams.
   What is the mass of the parcel? *423 g*
4. In a computer game Rita scores 7900 points, and David scores just 7 fewer.
   How many points does David score? *7893*
5. How many five-pence coins make £4.95? *99*
6. A theatre seats 684 people, with room for 26 people to stand.
   How many people are there in the theatre audience when it is full? *710*
7. In a certain country the tallest mountain is 4200 metres high, and the second tallest is 40 metres less.
   How high is the second tallest mountain? *4160 m*
8. Sonia and Steven have stamp collections. Steven has 670 stamps, but Sonia has twice as many. How many stamps does Sonia have? *1340*

4.7 Looking back (a)

Name ____________________

Date ____________________

		Answers
1	How much is 27 more than 938?	
2	Divide 185 by 5.	
3	In a telephone survey 5800 people were asked whether they thought the Earth was round or flat. Just 6 thought the Earth was flat. How many of them thought the Earth was round?	
4	Double 770.	
5	What is the time 20 minutes after 3.55?	
6	What is the sum of 174 and 43?	
7	Subtract 30 from 6500.	
8	One lunchtime a sandwich shop sold 590 sandwiches. How many slices of bread are used to make 590 sandwiches?	
9	How many 5s are there in 355?	
10	How many minutes are there between 8.40 a.m. and a quarter past 10 the same morning?	

4.7 Looking back (b)

Name ____________________

Date ____________________

		Answers
1	What is double 980?	
2	What time is it a quarter of an hour before five to 7?	
3	Ali has £4.65 in five-pence coins. How many coins is that?	
4	Add 82 and 555.	
5	What is 5 less than 9200?	
6	Divide 515 by 5.	
7	Sofie and Jim played a game. Sofie scored 846 points, but Jim scored 38 more. How many points did Jim score?	
8	How many minutes are there between 6.30 p.m. and 8.25 the same evening?	
9	Take 90 away from 7800.	
10	What is twice 860?	

4.7 Looking forward

Subtract a one-digit number from a three-digit multiple of 10

• 370 subtract 8	*362*
• 140 subtract 2	*138*
• 990 subtract 5	*985*
• 560 subtract 9	*551*
• 810 subtract 4	*806*
• 630 subtract 7	*623*

Multiply a two-digit multiple of 10 by 4

• 50 multiplied by 4	*200*
• 80 multiplied by 4	*320*
• 20 multiplied by 4	*80*
• 60 multiplied by 4	*240*
• 90 multiplied by 4	*360*
• 70 multiplied by 4	*280*

Double two-digit numbers

• double 32	*64*
• double 71	*142*
• double 26	*52*
• double 57	*114*
• double 48	*96*
• double 89	*178*

Double three-digit multiples of 10

• double 310	*620*
• double 470	*940*
• double 290	*580*
• double 840	*1680*
• double 550	*1100*
• double 630	*1260*

Divide a four-digit multiple of 100 or 1000 by 2

• 4000 divided by 2	*2000*
• 3600 divided by 2	*1800*
• 9000 divided by 2	*4500*
• 7000 divided by 2	*3500*
• 6300 divided by 2	*3150*
• 1500 divided by 2	*750*

Halve a three-digit multiple of 10

• one half of 620	*310*
• one half of 470	*235*
• one half of 380	*190*
• one half of 590	*295*
• one half of 830	*415*
• one half of 750	*375*

5.1 Addition

Content

- addition of (i) a three-digit multiple of 100 to a three-digit number (carrying to thousands, answer greater than 1000), and (ii) a three-digit multiple of 10 to a three-digit number (carrying to either hundreds or thousands)

Helpful knowledge and skills

- be able to add two three-digit multiples of 100 or two two-digit multiples of 10
- be able to add a two-digit or three-digit multiple of 10 to a three-digit multiple of 100

EXAMPLE

Add together 625 and 600

STRATEGY Near 600

625 + 600 = (600 + 25) + 600	• split to 600
= (600 + 600) + 25	• reorder and regroup
= 1200 + 25	• add
= 1225	• add

EXAMPLE

Find the sum of 390 and 437

STRATEGY Parts (hundreds, tens and units)

390 + 437 = (300 + 90) + (400 + 30 + 7)	• split to hundreds, tens and units
= (300 + 400) + (90 + 30) + 7	• reorder and regroup
= 700 + 120 + 7	• add
= 827	• add

STRATEGY Near 400

390 + 437 = (390 + 10) + 437 – 10	• adjust to 400 and balance
= 400 + 427	• add and subtract
= 827	• add

SHARE AND DISCUSS

Add 435 to 900

I changed the 900 to 1000 and added it to 435. Then I subtracted 100.

STRATEGY Near 1000

1 Calculate 324 add 800. *1124*

2 Calculate 500 plus 778. *1278*

3 What is 400 plus 991? *1391*

4 Find the total of 846 and 600. *1446*

5 What is the sum of 700 and 567? *1267*

6 Add together 900 and 812. *1712*

SHARE AND SYMBOLISE

What is the total of 254 and 160?

Take off 54 and you have 200. Take off 60 and you have 100. Add them together and you have 300. Then add 60 and 50 and 4 to make 414.

STRATEGY Parts (hundreds, tens and units)

$$254 + 160 = 200 + 100 + 54 + 60$$
$$= 300 + 60 + 50 + 4$$
$$= 414$$

1 What is the answer to 230 plus 383? *613*

2 Add 379 to 560. *939*

3 What is the sum of 495 and 270? *765*

4 Find the sum of 160 and 281. *441*

5 What is the answer to 790 add 197? *987*

6 Find the answer to 354 plus 450. *804*

PRACTISE AND DISCUSS

1 Add 270 to 695. *965*

2 Calculate 832 add 400. *1232*

3 What is the sum of 449 and 170? *619*

4 Calculate 461 plus 460. *921*

5 What is the answer to 500 plus 886? *1386*

6 What is the answer to 700 add 954? *1654*

7 Find the total of 370 and 333. *703*

8 Find the answer to 588 plus 270. *858*

9 What is the sum of 927 and 400? *1327*

10 Find the sum of 600 and 669. *1269*

5.2 Subtraction

Content

- subtraction of a two-digit number from a three-digit multiple of 10

Helpful knowledge and skills

- be able to subtract a two-digit number from a three-digit multiple of 100
- be able to subtract a two-digit multiple of 10 from a three-digit multiple of 10

EXAMPLE

What is 420 take away 35?

STRATEGY Parts (match tens)

$420 - 35 = 420 - (20 + 15)$	• split to match tens
$= (420 - 20) - 15$	• regroup
$= 400 - 15$	• subtract
$= 385$	• subtract

STRATEGY Parts (tens and units)

$420 - 35 = 420 - (30 + 5)$	• split to tens and units
$= (420 - 30) - 5$	• regroup
$= 390 - 5$	• subtract
$= 385$	• subtract

STRATEGY Parts (hundreds and tens)

$420 - 35 = (400 + 20) - 35$	• split to hundreds and tens
$= (400 - 35) + 20$	• reorder and regroup
$= 365 + 20$	• subtract
$= 385$	• add

SHARE AND DISCUSS

Subtract 51 from 540

I took the 40 from the 51, leaving 11. Then I took 11 off 500 to make 489.

STRATEGY Parts (match tens)

1 Subtract 75 from 360. *285*

2 What is 850 take away 97? *753*

3 From 170 take 84 away. *86*

4 What is the difference between 66 and 330? *264*

5 What is 950 minus 76? *874*

6 What is 92 less than 310? *218*

SHARE AND SYMBOLISE

What is 42 less than 420?

420 take away 40 is 380. Take away 2 is 378.

STRATEGY Parts (tens and units)

$$\begin{aligned} 420 - 42 &= 420 - 40 - 2 \\ &= 380 - 2 \\ &= 378 \end{aligned}$$

1 Subtract 57 from 630. *573*

2 Take 81 away from 230. *149*

3 What is 710 minus 69? *641*

4 Reduce 440 by 62. *378*

5 What is 540 take away 86? *454*

6 What is the difference between 820 and 74? *746*

PRACTISE AND DISCUSS

1 Take 87 away from 510. *423*

2 What is 430 minus 48? *382*

3 Subtract 96 from 370. *274*

4 What is 72 less than 730? *658*

5 From 750 take 68 away. *682*

6 What is the difference between 54 and 820? *766*

7 What is 510 minus 39? *471*

8 Subtract 88 from 260. *172*

9 What is 620 take away 94? *526*

10 Reduce 540 by 71. *469*

5.3 Investigating addition

COLLECT DATA

□ 6 3 + □ 0 0 = □ □ □ □

Give two examples:

463 + 800 = 1263
763 + 600 = 1363

463 + 800 = 1263	763 + 600 = 1363	863 + 200 = 1063
563 + 500 = 1063	963 + 200 = 1163	663 + 800 = 1463

Record children's examples on the board and keep for next lesson.

SORT AND ORDER DATA

Put the examples from the last lesson ready on the board.

Draw the sorting grid on the board.

Sort and order the examples in the grid. Leave gaps where necessary.
(The examples above are shown in shaded boxes.)

Complete the grid.

Answers should have four digits. The light diagonal shading shows answers with three digits. These may be completed later.

Second number	First number								
	163	263	363	463	563	663	763	863	963
100									1063
200								1063	1163
300							1063	1163	1263
400						1063	1163	1263	1363
500					1063	1163	1263	1363	1463
600				1063	1163	1263	1363	1463	1563
700			1063	1163	1263	1363	1463	1563	1663
800		1063	1163	1263	1363	1463	1563	1663	1763
900	1063	1163	1263	1363	1463	1563	1663	1763	1863

Keep the completed grid for the next lesson.

SEARCH FOR PATTERNS

Put the grid from the last lesson ready on the board.

Ask the children to describe a pattern in the table.

A response may be: 'The top numbers are all 1063'.
List some additions to help them see why this happens.

163 + 900 = 1063
263 + 800 = 1063
363 + 700 = 1063
463 + 600 = 1063
563 + 500 = 1063
636 + 400 = 1063
763 + 300 = 1063

Why are these answers all 1063?

You may need to help them by asking:
- *In what ways are the additions different?*
- *In what ways are the additions the same?*
- *Why do the answers stay the same?*

The first numbers increase by 100.
The second numbers decrease by 100.
The answers are always 1063.
Increasing one number by 100 and decreasing the other by the same amount leaves the answer the same.

5.3 Mathematics problem: Fractions and percentages

Content

- calculating simple fractions and percentages of a quantity

EXAMPLE

What is a third of 36? 12

2+3= Picture 36 as the whole:

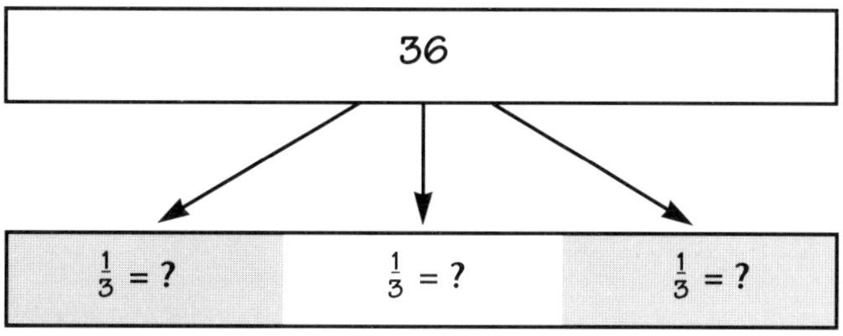

Divide the whole by the number of parts.

1 What is a fifth of 30? 6

2 Calculate a sixth of 42. 7

3 What is one-tenth of 200? 20

4 Calculate one-third of 45. 15

5 What is a fifth of 125? 25

6 Calculate one-eighth of 120. 15

EXAMPLE

What is 25% of 80? 20

2+3= Picture a circular whole for 80 (100%):

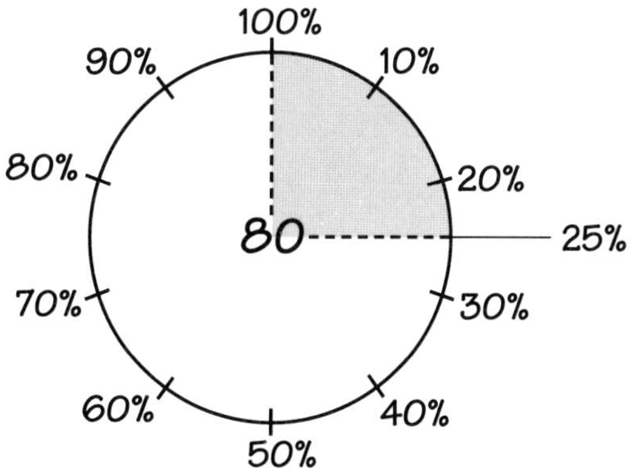

See the simple fraction ($\frac{1}{4}$) and divide by the number of parts.

1 Find 50% of 50. 25

2 What is 25% of 48? 12

3 Calculate 10% of 320. 32

4 Work out $33\frac{1}{3}$% of 60. 20

5 What is 20% of 25? 5

6 Calculate 5% of 120. 6

5.4 Multiplication

Content

- multiplication of a two-digit number by 4

Helpful knowledge and skills

- know 4 times table
- be able to multiply a two-digit multiple of 10 by 4
- be able to subtract a one-digit number from a three-digit multiple of 10
- be able to double a two-digit number
- be able to double a three-digit multiple of 10

EXAMPLE

What is 68 times 4?

STRATEGY Parts (tens and units)

$68 \times 4 = (60 + 8) \times 4$	• split to tens and units
$= (60 \times 4) + (8 \times 4)$	• regroup (distributive law)
$= 240 + 32$	• multiply
$= 272$	• add

STRATEGY Parts (factor of 2)

$68 \times 4 = 68 \times 2 \times 2$	• split to factor of 2
$= 136 \times 2$	• double
$= 272$	• double

STRATEGY Near 70

$68 \times 4 = (70 - 2) \times 4$	• adjust to 70 and balance
$= (70 \times 4) - (2 \times 4)$	• regroup (distributive law)
$= 280 - 8$	• multiply
$= 272$	• subtract

SHARE AND DISCUSS

Multiply 39 by 4

I multiplied 4 by 9 and that made 36. 4 times 30 equals 120. 120 add 36 equals 156.

STRATEGY Parts (tens and units)

1 Multiply 57 by 4. *228*

2 What is the product of 44 and 4? *176*

3 Calculate 93 multiplied by 4. *372*

4 How much is 78 multiplied by 4? *312*

5 What is 49 multiplied by 4? *196*

6 What is 4 times 85? *340*

SHARE AND SYMBOLISE

How much is 63 multiplied by 4?

I doubled 63 to make 126. Double it again gives the answer 252.

STRATEGY Parts (factor of 2)

$$
\begin{aligned}
63 \times 4 &= 63 \times 2 \times 2 \\
&= 126 \times 2 \\
&= 252
\end{aligned}
$$

1 Multiply 4 by 83. *332*

2 What is 4 times 37? *148*

3 Multiply 56 by 4. *224*

4 What is the product of 97 and 4? *388*

5 Calculate 65 times 4. *260*

6 How much is 74 multiplied by 4? *296*

PRACTISE AND DISCUSS

1 Multiply 4 by 46. *184*

2 What is 4 times 96? *384*

3 Multiply 88 by 4. *352*

4 What is the answer to 74 times 4? *296*

5 Calculate 48 multiplied by 4. *192*

6 How much is 87 times 4? *348*

7 Calculate 4 times 95. *380*

8 What is the product of 66 and 4? *264*

9 What is 79 multiplied by 4? *316*

10 What is 55 times 4? *220*

5.5 Division

Content

- halving and division by 2 of a four-digit multiple of 10 less than 2000

Helpful knowledge and skills

- be able to halve and divide by 2 a three-digit multiple of 10
- be able to halve and divide by 2 a three-digit or four-digit multiple of 100
- be able to halve and divide by 2 a four-digit multiple of 1000

EXAMPLE

What is half of 1500?

STRATEGY Parts (thousands and hundreds)

$\frac{1}{2}$ of 1500 = $\frac{1}{2}$ of (1000 + 500)	• split to thousands and hundreds
= $\frac{1}{2}$ of 1000 + $\frac{1}{2}$ of 500	• regroup (distributive law)
= 500 + 250	• halves
= 750	• add

STRATEGY Near 1600

$\frac{1}{2}$ of 1500 = $\frac{1}{2}$ of (1600 – 100)	• adjust to 1600 and balance
= $\frac{1}{2}$ of 1600 – $\frac{1}{2}$ of 100	• regroup (distributive law)
= 800 – 50	• halves
= 750	• subtract

EXAMPLE

Divide 1380 by 2

STRATEGY Parts

1380 ÷ 2 = (1200 + 180) ÷ 2	• split to easier numbers
= (1200 ÷ 2) + (180 ÷ 2)	• regroup (distributive law)
= 600 + 90	• divide
= 690	• add

SHARE AND DISCUSS

What is half of 1800?

Half of 1000 is 500.
Half of 800 is 400.
500 and 400 make 900.

STRATEGY **Parts (thousands and hundreds)**

1 Find 1200 divided by 2. *600*

2 What is 1900 divided by 2? *950*

3 What is half of 1100? *550*

4 Divide 1400 into 2 equal parts. *700*

5 What is half of 1600? *800*

6 What is 1700 divided by 2? *850*

SHARE AND SYMBOLISE

Divide 1720 by 2

I took 120 away from 1720 to give 1600. 16 divided by 2 is 8, so for 1600 divided by 2 I put on two noughts to make 800. I then added 60 to make 860.

STRATEGY **Near 1600 and Parts (factor of 100)**

$$
\begin{aligned}
1720 \div 2 &= (1600 + 120) \div 2 \\
&= (1600 \div 2) + (120 \div 2) \\
&= (16 \times 100 \div 2) + (120 \div 2) \\
&= (8 \times 100) + (120 \div 2) \\
&= 800 + 60 \\
&= 860
\end{aligned}
$$

1 Find 1860 divided by 2. *930*

2 Divide 1220 into 2 equal parts. *610*

3 Halve 1580. *790*

4 Find a half of 1740. *870*

5 What is 1450 divided by 2? *725*

6 Calculate 1930 divided by 2. *965*

PRACTISE AND DISCUSS

1 Find 1360 divided by 2. *680*

2 What is 1500 divided by 2? *750*

3 How many is half of 1180? *590*

4 What is 1250 divided by 2? *625*

5 How many lots of 2 add up to 1470? *735*

6 How many is half of 1690? *845*

7 Divide 1720 into 2 equal parts. *860*

8 Calculate 1910 divided by 2. *955*

9 How many 2s are there in 1530? *765*

10 Find a half of 1820. *910*

5.6 Investigating doubling

COLLECT DATA

Start with the same number.

□□ doubled is □□, doubled is □□

□□ multiplied by 4 is □□

Give one example:

13 doubled is 26, doubled is 52
13 multiplied by 4 is 52

Record children's examples on the board.

13 doubled is 26, doubled is 52 13 multiplied by 4 is 52	24 doubled is 48, doubled is 96 24 multiplied by 4 is 96
17 doubled is 34, doubled is 68 17 multiplied by 4 is 68	15 doubled is 30, doubled is 60 15 multiplied by 4 is 60

- *What do you see happening?* The answers at the end are the same.
- *Will it always work?* Test with some more examples using larger two-digit numbers.
- *Why does it work?* Because $2 \times 2 = 4$.

COLLECT DATA

Start with the same number.

□□ doubled is □□, doubled is □□, doubled is □□□

□□ multiplied by 8 is □□□

Give one example:

13 doubled is 26, doubled is 52, doubled is 104
13 multiplied by 8 is 104

Record children's examples on the board.

13 doubled is 26, doubled is 52, doubled is 104 13 multiplied by 8 is 104
15 doubled is 30, doubled is 60, doubled is 120 15 multiplied by 8 is 120

- *What do you see happening?* The answers at the end are the same.
- *Will it always work?* Test with some more examples using larger two-digit numbers.
- *Why does it work?* Because $2 \times 2 \times 2 = 8$.
- *How can you use doubling to help you multiply by 16?*
- *What other multiplications can you do by repeated doubling?*

36 apples are cut into quarter pieces. How many pieces of apple are there altogether? *144*

Picture a whole circle in quarters:

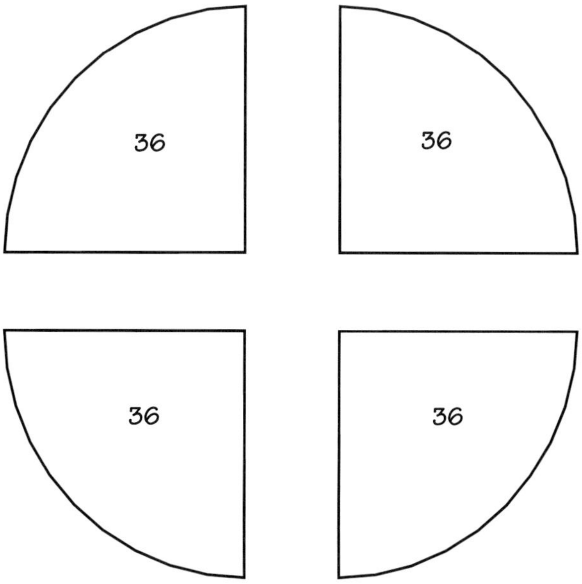

Think of 36 of each part.

1. A car 482 centimetres long is pulling a trailer which with the tow is 340 centimetres long. What is the total length of car, tow and trailer? *822 cm*
2. 570 people were asked about having a pet. 84 of them did not have any pets. How many people had pets? *486*
3. One burger costs 68 pence. How much is it for 4 such burgers? *£2.72*
4. A school has 1140 pupils. There are exactly the same number of boys as girls. How many boys are there? *570*
5. Haroon scores 574 points in a game, and gets 600 bonus points. How many points is his total score? *1174*
6. There are 4 rows of chairs with 47 chairs in each row. How many chairs is that altogether? *188*
7. A prize of £1470 is shared equally between 2 people. How much do they each get? *£735*
8. Of the 330 children in a school, 58 go home for lunch. How many stay at school? *272*

5.7 Looking back (a)

Name ____________________

Date ____________________

		Answers
1	Calculate one-third of 72.	
2	Reduce 450 by 84.	
3	On a two-week drive to clean up litter, 460 pieces of litter were picked up in the first week, and 374 in the second week. How many pieces of litter was that altogether?	
4	How much is it for 4 sandwiches at 98 pence each?	
5	What is 1070 divided by 2?	
6	In a survey of 80 children, 25% said they liked yoghurt. How many children liked yoghurt?	
7	Multiply 76 by 4.	
8	Divide 1520 by 2.	
9	Two classes collected silver paper for charity. One class collected 820 pieces in one week. The other class collected 66 fewer pieces. How many pieces did the second class collect?	
10	Add 800 to 743.	

5.7 Looking back (b)

Name ____________________

Date ____________________

		Answers
1	What is 540 minus 92?	
2	Calculate one-sixth of 72.	
3	A single piece of paper when folded makes a 4-page booklet. How many pages will there be when 47 pieces of paper are folded?	
4	What is the sum of 928 and 560?	
5	A sandwich shop buys 85 loaves of bread to make into sandwiches. There are 16 slices of bread in each loaf, which is 1360 slices altogether. How many full sandwiches can they make?	
6	What is 28 subtracted from 710?	
7	What is 4 times 69?	
8	Some jeans are reduced by 20% in a sale. They usually cost £20. What is 20% of £20?	
9	Add 177 to 650.	
10	Calculate a half of 1850.	

5.7 Looking forward

Split a four-digit number in various ways

• 3459 is 3000 and what?	*459*
• 4877 is 700 and what?	*4177*
• 9591 is 91 and what?	*9500*
• 8356 is 350 and what?	*8006*
• 5938 is 438 and what?	*5500*
• 2264 is 250 and what?	*2014*

Add a four-digit multiple of 10 to a three-digit multiple of 100 (without carrying)

• 3420 add 200	*3620*
• 6280 add 700	*6980*
• 4510 add 400	*4910*
• 8150 add 800	*8950*
• 2390 add 500	*2890*
• 9670 add 100	*9770*

Subtract a one-digit number from a three-digit multiple of 10

• 240 subtract 8	*232*
• 510 subtract 2	*508*
• 390 subtract 5	*385*
• 650 subtract 9	*641*
• 820 subtract 3	*817*
• 760 subtract 7	*753*

Subtract a three-digit multiple of 100 from a four-digit multiple of 1000

• 5000 subtract 700	*4300*
• 6000 subtract 200	*5800*
• 1000 subtract 300	*700*
• 9000 subtract 800	*8200*
• 2000 subtract 500	*1500*
• 4000 subtract 900	*3100*

Multiply a two-digit multiple of 10 by 3

• 70 multiplied by 3	*210*
• 40 multiplied by 3	*120*
• 20 multiplied by 3	*60*
• 90 multiplied by 3	*270*
• 50 multiplied by 3	*150*
• 80 multiplied by 3	*240*

Divide a two-digit number less than 50 by a one-digit number, answer with remainder

• 37 divided by 3	*12 rem 1*
• 24 divided by 5	*4 rem 4*
• 16 divided by 9	*1 rem 7*
• 43 divided by 4	*10 rem 3*
• 32 divided by 6	*5 rem 2*
• 27 divided by 7	*3 rem 6*

6.1 Addition

Content

- addition of (i) a four-digit multiple of 10 to a two-digit multiple of 10 (carrying to hundreds), and (ii) a four-digit multiple of 10 to a three-digit multiple of a 100 (carrying to thousands)

Helpful knowledge and skills

- know how to split a four-digit number in a variety of ways
- be able to add a four-digit multiple of 10 to a three-digit multiple of 100 (no carrying)

.... EXAMPLE ....

What is 2840 plus 80?

STRATEGY **Near 100**

2840 + 80	= 2840 + (100 − 20)	• adjust to 100 and balance
	= (2840 + 100) − 20	• regroup
	= 2940 − 20	• add
	= 2920	• subtract

.... EXAMPLE ....

Add together 800 and 1730

STRATEGY **Parts (complement to 1000)**

800 + 1730	= 800 + (200 + 1530)	• split to make up to 1000
	= (800 + 200) + 1530	• regroup
	= 1000 + 1530	• add
	= 2530	• add

STRATEGY **Parts (thousands, hundreds and tens)**

800 + 1730	= 800 + (1000 + 700 + 30)	• split to thousands, hundreds and tens
	= 1000 + (800 + 700) + 30	• reorder and regroup
	= 1000 + 1500 + 30	• add
	= 2530	• add

SHARE AND DISCUSS

What is the total of 3860 and 90?

I made 90 into 100 and took 10 off 3860 to give 3850. Then I added 100 to 3850 to make 3950.

STRATEGY **Near 1000**

1 Find the sum of 3750 and 70. 3820

2 Find the total of 80 and 5590. 5670

3 Find the answer to 60 add 9260. 9320

4 What is 6870 plus 80? 6950

5 Add together 90 and 4650. 4740

6 What is the sum of 40 and 2480? 2520

SHARE AND SYMBOLISE

Add together 400 and 6720

Take 120 from 6720 gives 6600, and add 400 gives 7000. Then add the 120 to give 7120.

STRATEGY **Parts (complement to 7000)**

$$400 + 6720 = 400 + 6600 + 120$$
$$= 7000 + 120$$
$$= 7120$$

1 What is 400 add 6930? 7330

2 Add 7650 to 800. 8450

3 Calculate 900 plus 8240. 9140

4 Calculate 300 add 1870. 2170

5 What is the answer to 8760 add 700? 9460

6 What is the answer to 600 plus 4580? 5180

PRACTISE AND DISCUSS

1 Find the sum of 30 and 9390. 9420

2 What is 200 add 1890? 2090

3 Find the total of 500 and 7920. 8420

4 Calculate 5240 plus 70. 5310

5 Find the answer to 7650 add 80. 7730

6 What is 100 plus 5930? 6030

7 Calculate 60 add 3580. 3640

8 Add together 4950 and 900. 5850

9 What is the answer to 90 plus 2840? 2930

10 What is the sum of 6770 and 600? 7370

6.2 Subtraction

Content

- subtraction of (i) a three-digit multiple of 100 from a four-digit multiple of 10, and (ii) a two-digit multiple of 10 from a four-digit multiple of 10

Helpful knowledge and skills

- be able to subtract a two-digit multiple of 10 from a four-digit multiple of 1000
- be able to subtract a three-digit multiple of 100 from a four-digit multiple of 1000

EXAMPLE

Subtract 800 from 5550

STRATEGY **Parts (match hundreds)**

5550 – 800 = 5550 – 500 – 300	• split to match hundreds
= 5050 – 300	• subtract
= 4750	• subtract

STRATEGY **Near 1000**

5550 – 800 = 5550 – 1000 + 200	• adjust to 1000 and balance
= 4550 + 200	• subtract
= 4750	• add

EXAMPLE

What is 2760 minus 90?

STRATEGY **Near 100**

2760 – 90 = 2760 – 100 + 10	• adjust to 100 and balance
= 2660 + 10	• subtract
= 2670	• add

SHARE AND DISCUSS

What is 4320 take away 400?

> First I took away 300, which left 4020. Then I took away 100, leaving 3920.

STRATEGY Parts (match hundreds)

1. Subtract 500 from 7220. *6720*
2. What is 6450 take away 700? *5750*
3. Reduce 3470 by 800. *2670*
4. What is 4690 minus 900? *3790*
5. What is 300 subtracted from 8180? *7880*
6. What is the difference between 600 and 2330? *1730*

SHARE AND SYMBOLISE

What is 3110 minus 90?

> I made 90 into 100, and took 100 from 3110 to make 3010. Then I added 10 to make 3020.

STRATEGY Near 100

$$3110 - 90 = 3110 - 100 + 10$$
$$= 3010 + 10$$
$$= 3020$$

1. Take 70 away from 4150. *4080*
2. What is 6440 minus 50? *6390*
3. Subtract 40 from 9210. *9170*
4. What is the difference between 3650 and 90? *3560*
5. What is 1220 minus 80? *1140*
6. What is 60 less than 7730? *7670*

PRACTISE AND DISCUSS

1. Take 600 away from 7580. *6980*
2. What is 3760 minus 70? *3690*
3. Subtract 30 from 9920. *9890*
4. What is 6150 take away 400? *5750*
5. From 2480 take 900 away. *1580*
6. What is the difference between 90 and 5320? *5230*
7. What is 4610 minus 800? *3810*
8. What is 70 less than 4220? *4150*
9. Reduce 8450 by 600. *7850*
10. What is the difference between 6110 and 200? *5910*

6.3 Investigating addition

COLLECT DATA

2+3=

3	6	☐	0	+	☐	0	=	☐	☐	5	0

Give two examples:

3620 + 30 = 3650
3670 + 80 = 3750

3620 + 30 = 3650	3670 + 80 = 3750	3640 + 10 = 3650
3660 + 90 = 3750	3630 + 20 = 3650	3690 + 60 = 3750

Record children's examples on the board and keep for next lesson.

SEARCH FOR PATTERNS

2+3= Put the examples from the last lesson ready on the board.

Ask the children to describe a pattern in the answers.

A response may be: 'The answers are either 3650 or 3750'.
List some additions and underline the thousands and hundreds to draw attention to 'changes'.

3620 + 30 = 3650	3670 + 80 = 3750
3640 + 10 = 3650	3660 + 90 = 3750
3630 + 20 = 3650	3690 + 60 = 3750

Why are the answers either 3650 or 3750?
You may need to help them by asking:

- *What makes the 600s stay as 600s?* There is no carry from the tens, for example:
  3620 + 30 = 3600 + 20 + 30 = 3600 + 50 = 3650
- *What makes the 600s change to 700s?* There is a carry from the tens, for example:
  3670 + 80 = 3600 + 70 + 80 = 3600 + 150 = 3750

COLLECT DATA

2+3=

5	☐	8	0	+	☐	0	0	=	☐	3	☐	0

Give two examples:

5180 + 200 = 5380
5680 + 700 = 6380

5180 + 200 = 5380	5680 + 700 = 6380	5080 + 300 = 5380
5980 + 400 = 6380	5880 + 500 = 6380	5780 + 600 = 6380

Record children's examples on the board and keep for next lesson.

SEARCH FOR PATTERNS

2+3= Put the examples from the last lesson ready on the board.

Ask the children to describe a pattern in the answers.

A response may be: 'The answers are either 5380 or 6380'.
List some additions to help them see this.

5180 + 200 = 5380	5680 + 700 = 6380
5080 + 300 = 5380	5980 + 400 = 6380
	5880 + 500 = 6380
	5780 + 600 = 6380

Why are the answers either 5380 or 6380?
You may need to help them by asking:

- *What makes the 5000 change to 6000?* There is a carry from the hundreds, for example:
  5680 + 700 = 5000 + 680 + 700 = 5000 + 1380 = 6380
- *What makes the 5000 stay as 5000?* There is no carry from the hundreds, for example:
  5180 + 200 = 5000 + 180 + 200 = 5000 + 380 = 5380

6.3 Mathematics problem: Negative numbers

Content

- addition and subtraction (as difference) with negative numbers

EXAMPLE

Add 6 to minus 3

3 or +3

2+3= Picture pluses and minuses:

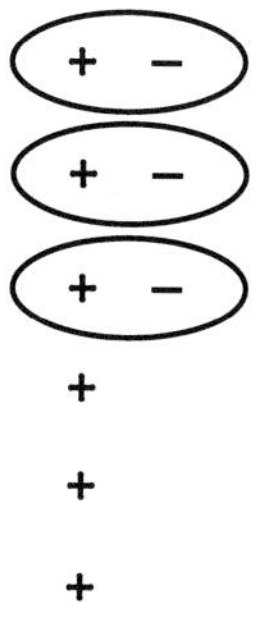

Couple a plus with a minus to balance each other.

1 Add 3 to minus 6. *−3*

2 What is negative 4 plus negative 5? *−9*

3 Add together minus 4, plus 5 and minus 3. *−2*

4 What is negative 6 plus 10 plus negative 3? *+1*

5 Add together negative 5, negative 7 and positive 4. *−8*

6 What is the sum of plus 12, minus 17 and minus 19? *−24*

EXAMPLE

What is the difference between 6 and minus 3?

9

2+3= Picture a number line:

Locate both numbers on a number line with zero.

1 What is the difference between 2 and minus 7? *9*

2 What is the difference between 4 and negative 2? *6*

3 What is the difference between negative 3 and negative 5? *2*

4 What is the difference between minus 6 and plus 10? *16*

5 What is the difference between negative 12 and positive 5? *17*

6 What is the difference between minus 60 and minus 100? *40*

6.4 Multiplication

Content

- multiplication of a two-digit number by 3

Helpful knowledge and skills

- know 3 times table
- be able to multiply a two-digit multiple of 10 by 3
- be able to subtract a one-digit number from a three-digit multiple of 10
- be able to subtract a two-digit number from a three-digit multiple of 10

EXAMPLE

Multiply 69 by 3

STRATEGY Parts (tens and units)

$69 \times 3 = (60 + 9) \times 3$	• split to tens and units
$= (60 \times 3) + (9 \times 3)$	• regroup (distributive law)
$= 180 + 27$	• multiply
$= 207$	• add

STRATEGY Near 70

$69 \times 3 = (70 - 1) \times 3$	• adjust to 70 and balance
$= (70 \times 3) - (1 \times 3)$	• regroup (distributive law)
$= 210 - 3$	• multiply
$= 207$	• subtract

STRATEGY Parts (known facts)

$69 \times 3 = (30 + 30 + 9) \times 3$	• split to easier numbers
$= (30 \times 3) + (30 \times 3) + (9 \times 3)$	• regroup (distributive law)
$= 90 + 90 + 27$	• multiply
$= 180 + 27$	• add
$= 207$	• add

SHARE AND DISCUSS

What is 64 times 3?

First I worked out 60 times 3. 6 times 3 equals 18, and then add the 0 to make 180. Then 4 times 3 is 12. Add 12 to 180 to make 192.

STRATEGY Parts (tens and units)

1	Multiply 88 by 3.	*264*	4	How much is 39 multiplied by 3?	*117*
2	What is the answer to 74 times 3?	*222*	5	What is the product of 78 and 3?	*234*
3	Calculate 95 multiplied by 3.	*285*	6	What is 3 times 46?	*138*

SHARE AND SYMBOLISE

What is 58 multiplied by 3?

60 times 3 is 180. Take away 6 will equal 174.

STRATEGY Near 60

$$58 \times 3 = (60 \times 3) - (2 \times 3)$$
$$= 180 - 6$$
$$= 174$$

1	Multiply 3 by 44.	*132*	4	How much is 37 times 3?	*111*
2	What is 3 times 98?	*294*	5	Calculate the product of 85 and 3.	*255*
3	Multiply 65 by 3.	*195*	6	How much is 56 multiplied by 3?	*168*

PRACTISE AND DISCUSS

1	Multiply 3 by 36.	*108*	6	What is the product of 47 and 3?	*141*
2	What is 3 times 87?	*261*	7	Calculate 96 times 3.	*288*
3	Multiply 68 by 3.	*204*	8	How much is 38 multiplied by 3?	*114*
4	What is the answer to 76 times 3?	*228*	9	What is 79 multiplied by 3?	*237*
5	Calculate 94 multiplied by 3.	*282*	10	What is 49 times 3?	*147*

6.5 Division

Content

- division of a two-digit number greater than 50 and less than 100 by a one-digit number, answer with remainder

Helpful knowledge and skills

- know how to split a two-digit number in a variety of ways
- be able to divide a two-digit number less than 50 by a one-digit number

EXAMPLE

Divide 67 by 7. Give the answer with a remainder.

STRATEGY **Parts (known facts)**

67 ÷ 7 = (35 + 14 + 14 + 4) ÷ 7	• split to easier numbers
= (35 ÷ 7) + (14 ÷ 7) + (14 ÷ 7) + (4 ÷ 7)	• regroup (distributive law)
= 5 + 2 + 2 + 0 rem 4	• divide
= 9 rem 4	• add

STRATEGY **Parts (known facts)**

67 ÷ 7 = (49 + 18) ÷ 7	• split to easier numbers
= (49 ÷ 7) + (18 ÷ 7)	• regroup (distributive law)
= 7 + 2 rem 4	• divide
= 9 rem 4	• add

STRATEGY **Near 63**

67 ÷ 7 = (63 + 4) ÷ 7	• split to 63
= (63 ÷ 7) + (4 ÷ 7)	• regroup (distributive law)
= 9 + 0 rem 4	• divide
= 9 rem 4	• add

SHARE AND DISCUSS

What is 56 divided by 3? Give the answer with a remainder.

30 divided by 3 is 10. 24 divided by 3 is 8. Add 10 and 8 to get 18. 30 add 24 is 54 and 2 more is 56. The answer is 18 remainder 2.

STRATEGY Parts (known facts)

Give your answers with a remainder.

1. Divide 71 into 5 equal parts. *14 rem 1*
2. Calculate 87 divided by 7. *12 rem 3*
3. What is 89 divided by 8? *11 rem 1*
4. What is 67 divided by 4? *16 rem 3*
5. Divide 3 into 97. *32 rem 1*
6. Find 95 divided by 6. *15 rem 5*

SHARE AND SYMBOLISE

Divide 77 by 6, giving the answer with a remainder.

I took away 17 from 77 making 60, and divided that by 6 to get 10. Then I found how many 6s were in 17, which was 2 remainder 5. So the answer is 12 remainder 5.

STRATEGY Parts (known facts)

$$77 \div 6 = (60 + 17) \div 6$$
$$= (60 \div 6) + (17 \div 6)$$
$$= 10 + 2 \text{ remainder } 5$$
$$= 12 \text{ remainder } 5$$

Give your answers with a remainder.

1. What is 76 divided by 3? *25 rem 1*
2. Divide 62 by 5. *12 rem 2*
3. Calculate 85 divided by 4. *21 rem 1*
4. Find 79 divided by 7. *11 rem 2*
5. What is 83 divided by 9? *9 rem 2*
6. Divide 8 into 92. *11 rem 4*

PRACTISE AND DISCUSS

Give your answers with a remainder.

1. Find 94 divided by 7. *13 rem 3*
2. What is 86 divided by 5? *17 rem 1*
3. How many is 82 divided by 3? *27 rem 1*
4. Divide 88 by 6. *14 rem 4*
5. Find the answer to 96 divided by 9. *10 rem 6*
6. Find 73 divided by 4. *18 rem 1*
7. Calculate 78 divided by 9. *8 rem 6*
8. Find the answer to 93 divided by 5. *18 rem 3*
9. Calculate 74 divided by 8. *9 rem 2*
10. Divide 91 by 4. *22 rem 3*

6.6 Investigating division

COLLECT DATA

Use the same start number.

☐☐ ÷ 2 = ☐☐ remainder ☐

☐☐ ÷ 3 = ☐☐ remainder ☐

Give two examples:

42 ÷ 2 = 21 rem 0
42 ÷ 3 = 14 rem 0
46 ÷ 2 = 23 rem 0
46 ÷ 3 = 15 rem 1

42 ÷ 2 = 21 rem 0 42 ÷ 3 = 14 rem 0	46 ÷ 2 = 23 rem 0 46 ÷ 3 = 15 rem 1	47 ÷ 2 = 23 rem 1 47 ÷ 3 = 15 rem 2
38 ÷ 2 = 19 rem 0 38 ÷ 3 = 12 rem 2	59 ÷ 2 = 29 rem 1 59 ÷ 3 = 19 rem 2	69 ÷ 2 = 34 rem 1 69 ÷ 3 = 23 rem 0

Record children's examples on the board and keep for next lesson.

SORT AND ORDER DATA

Put the examples from the last lesson ready on the board. Draw the sorting grid on the board.

Sort and order the examples in the grid. Leave gaps where necessary.
(The examples above are shown in shaded boxes.) Complete the grid as far as 100.

		Divided by 3 leaves								
		remainder 0			**remainder 1**			**remainder 2**		
Divided by 2 leaves	**remainder 0**	0	6	12	4	10	16	2	8	14
		18	24	30	22	28	34	20	26	32
		36	42	48	40	46	52	38	44	50
		54	60	66	58	64	70	56	62	68
		72	78	84	76	82	88	74	80	86
		90	96		94	100		92		
	remainder 1	3	9	15	1	7	13	5	11	17
		21	27	33	19	25	31	23	29	35
		39	45	51	37	43	49	41	47	53
		57	63	69	55	61	67	59	65	71
		75	81	87	73	79	85	77	83	89
		93	99		91	97		95		

Keep the completed grid for the next lesson.

SEARCH FOR PATTERNS

Put the grid from the last lesson ready on the board.

Ask the children to describe a pattern in the grid.

A response may be: 'The numbers go up in 6s'.
List some divisions to help them see this.

6 ÷ 2 = 3 rem 0 6 ÷ 3 = 2 rem 0	18 ÷ 2 = 9 rem 0 18 ÷ 3 = 6 rem 0
12 ÷ 2 = 6 rem 0 12 ÷ 3 = 4 rem 0	24 ÷ 2 = 12 rem 0 30 ÷ 3 = 10 rem 0

Why do the numbers go up in 6s?

You may need to help them by asking:

- *What numbers divide into 6 with 0 remainder?* The numbers 1, 2, 3 and 6. These are known as divisors of 6.
- *Why do the numbers go up in 6s?* Because 6 divides by 2 and 3, and 12 which is 6 more will also divide by 2 and 3. So will 18, and so on.

6.6 Word problems

A tower 70 metres tall is built on top of a mountain. The height of the mountain above sea level is 4350 metres. What is the height above sea level of the top of the tower? 4420 m

2+3= Picture the tower on the mountain:

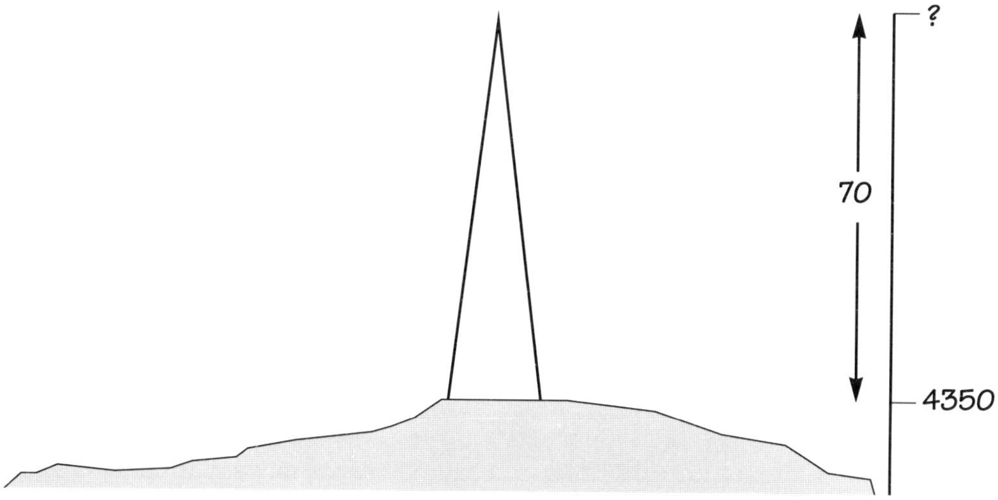

Think of the extra height.

1 Dale scores 2870 points in a game, and gets 600 bonus points. What is Dale's total score? *3470*

2 One burger costs 68 pence. How much is it for 3 such burgers? *£2.04*

3 There are 96 children in a tournament. They are put into groups of 5. How many groups are there, and how many children are left out? *19 rem 1*

4 A flock of migrating birds travels 3240 miles between their winter feeding place and their breeding ground. When they are passing over London they have 80 miles left to fly. How far have they travelled to that point? *3160 miles*

5 Some chairs are put out in 3 rows. There are 37 chairs in each row. How many chairs are there altogether? *111*

6 At the start of a journey a car's milometer shows a reading of 7480. The journey is 70 miles. What will the reading be at the end of the journey? *7550*

7 There are 73 children to be seated for lunch. Each dining table seats 6. How many full tables will be used, and how many children will be left over? *12 rem 1*

8 One day a theme park has 5670 visitors. The first 900 visitors are allowed in at half price. How many visitors pay full price? *4770*

6.7 Looking back (a)

Name ____________________

Date ____________________

		Answers
1	Divide 55 by 4, giving the answer with a remainder.	
2	What is 50 less than 3530?	
3	In a game Seph scores 5360 points and gets a bonus of 800. What is his total score?	
4	Multiply 3 by 84.	
5	What is the difference between –6 and 7?	
6	What is 67 multiplied by 3?	
7	There are 6 felt-tip pens in a packet. Sarah counts 69 pens. How many full packets can be made and how many pens will be in the partly filled one?	
8	Reduce 7590 by 700.	
9	One night in winter the temperature is –3 at sunset, and drops by another 5 degrees by dawn. What is the temperature at dawn?	
10	What is the sum of 9170 and 60?	

6.7 Looking back (b)

Name ____________________

Date ____________________

		Answers
1	Add –8 to 3.	
2	An expedition is arranged to the South Pole. From the starting camp to the Pole it is 5480 miles in total, but 800 of these are by boat. How many miles of travel are not by boat?	
3	What is 3 times 48?	
4	How many 8s are there in 79? What is the remainder?	
5	Calculate 7840 plus 90.	
6	One cold night the temperature is –5 degrees in Glasgow and –9 degrees in Edinburgh. Which city was colder, and by how many degrees?	
7	What is 80 less than 4010?	
8	3 sticks are laid end to end in a straight line. Each stick is 79 centimetres long. What is the total length?	
9	What is 92 divided by 7, giving the answer with a remainder?	
10	Add 500 to 2770.	

6.7 Looking all the way back (a)

Name _____

Date _____

		Answers
1	Annabel buys a computer for £870 and a printer for £520. How much does she pay altogether?	☐
2	There are 420 children in a school. 140 of them go on a school visit to a museum. How many do not go to the museum?	☐
3	What is the product of 60 and 30?	☐
4	What is one quarter of 152 kilometres?	☐
5	Ahmed sends three letters. The stamps cost 42p, 25p and 27p. What is the total cost of stamps for the three letters?	☐
6	Double 46.	☐
7	What is £15 601 to the nearest thousand pounds?	☐
8	Calculate 72 divided by 4.	☐
9	What number is half-way between 132 and 484?	☐
10	Add 276 to 53.	☐

Teaching Mental Maths Strategies 5

6.7 Looking all the way back (b)

Name _____

Date _____

		Answers
1	Subtract 370 from 826.	☐
2	What is 27 multiplied by 5?	☐
3	In a secondary school there are 351 boys and 580 girls. How many children are there altogether in the school?	☐
4	Divide 375 by 5.	☐
5	What is one-third of £69?	☐
6	What is the difference between 510 and 96?	☐
7	Carmen buys a second-hand car for £3700. She pays half of the price in cash. How much does she pay in cash?	☐
8	5320 tickets are sold for a pop concert. 700 tickets are left unsold. How many tickets were for sale altogether?	☐
9	A bottle of juice contains 55 centilitres. How many centilitres do 3 bottles contain altogether?	☐
10	What is 25% of 160 kilograms?	☐

Answers to Looking back

1.1 Looking back

a			
1	634	6	40
2	146	7	33
3	1440	8	8
4	$32\frac{1}{2}$	9	114
5	484	10	9
b			
1	61	6	51p
2	1140	7	18
3	60	8	2200
4	431	9	142
5	146	10	7 rem 2

1.8 Looking back

a			
1	1150	6	850
2	£18	7	435
3	335	8	370 cm
4	150	9	81
5	77	10	3200
b			
1	120	6	440
2	750 ml	7	$62\frac{1}{2}$
3	4200	8	2400
4	86	9	1840
5	1120 cm	10	670

2.7 Looking back

a			
1	132	6	328
2	750 cm	7	15 000 g
3	854	8	5616
4	£2275	9	£1.74
5	15	10	14
b			
1	6808	6	3149
2	156	7	923
3	$5\frac{1}{2}$ cm	8	19
4	657	9	3500 ml
5	13	10	118

3.7 Looking back

a			
1	96	6	6
2	7000	7	325
3	104	8	178
4	561	9	152
5	85	10	430
b			
1	92	6	4000
2	7	7	98p
3	144	8	290
4	88	9	126
5	235	10	175

4.7 Looking back

a			
1	965	6	217
2	37	7	6470
3	5794	8	1180
4	1540	9	71
5	4.15	10	95 min
b			
1	1960	6	103
2	6.40	7	884
3	93	8	115 min
4	637	9	7710
5	9195	10	1720

5.7 Looking back

a			
1	24	6	20
2	366	7	304
3	834	8	760
4	£3.92	9	754
5	535	10	1543
b			
1	448	6	682
2	12	7	276
3	188	8	£4
4	1488	9	827
5	680	10	925

6.7 Looking back

a			
1	13 rem 3	6	201
2	3480	7	11 rem 3
3	6160	8	6890
4	252	9	−8
5	13	10	9230
b			
1	−5	6	Ed. by 4
2	4680	7	3930
3	144	8	237 cm
4	9 rem 7	9	13 rem 1
5	7930	10	3270

6.7 Looking all the way back

a			
1	£1390	6	92
2	280	7	£16 000
3	1800	8	18
4	38 km	9	308
5	94p	10	329
b			
1	456	6	414
2	135	7	£1850
3	931	8	6020
4	75	9	165 cl
5	£23	10	40 kg

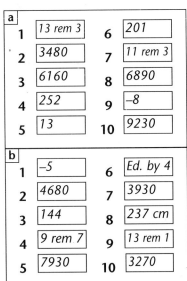